AF575962

SHORE LEAVE

SHORE LEAVE

Edited by Ryan Mungia
Essay by Jim Heimann

BOYO

"Give me something, O God, to divert me . . . so that I won't have to be alone with myself." —William Bradford Huie, *The Revolt of Mamie Stover*

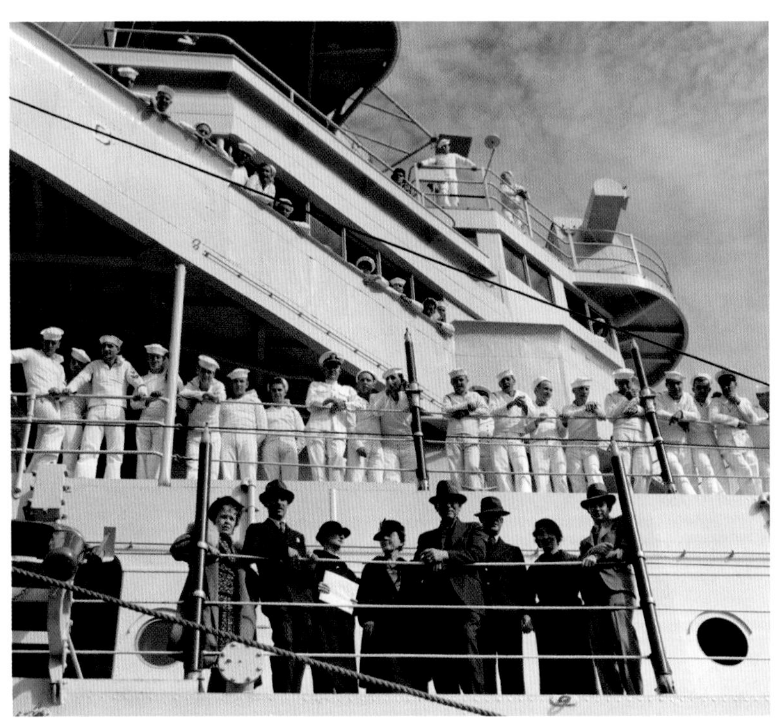

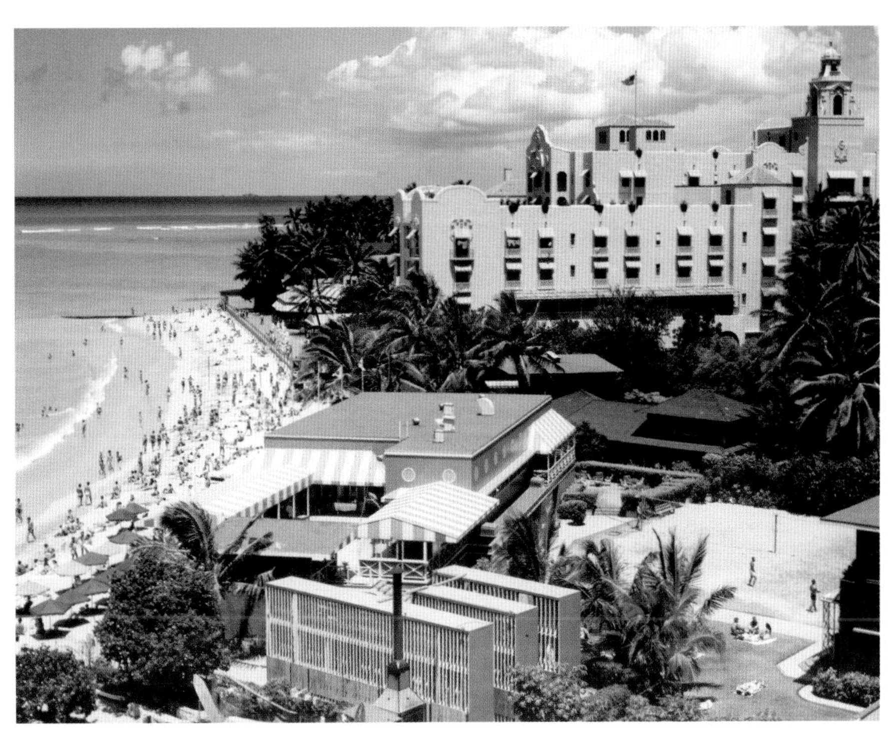

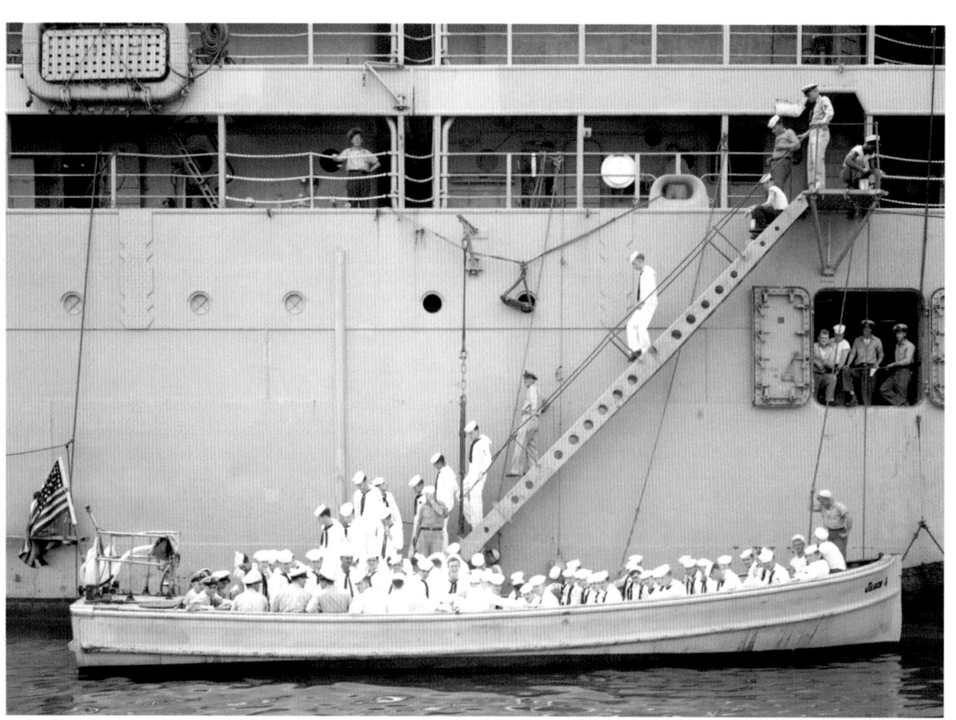

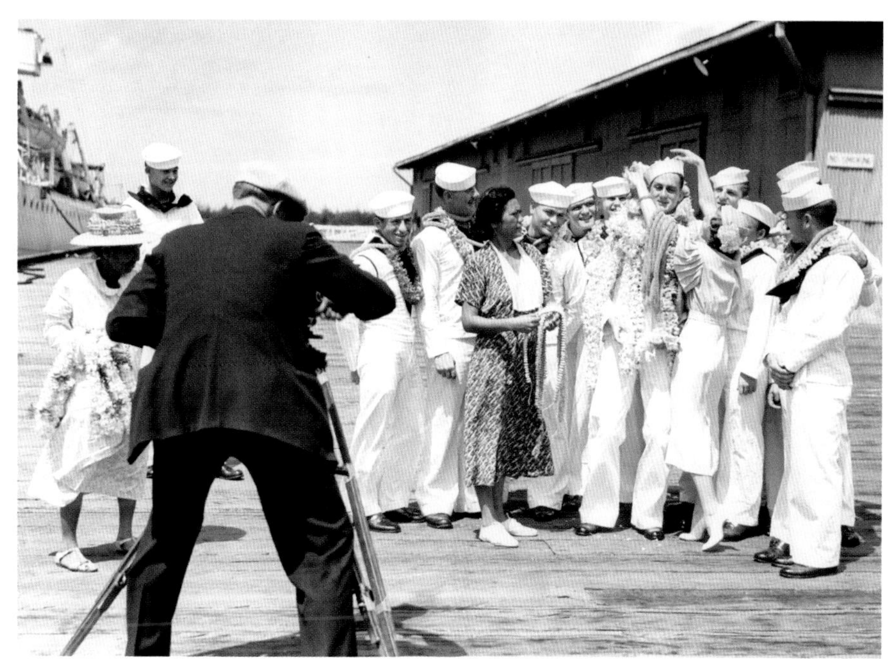

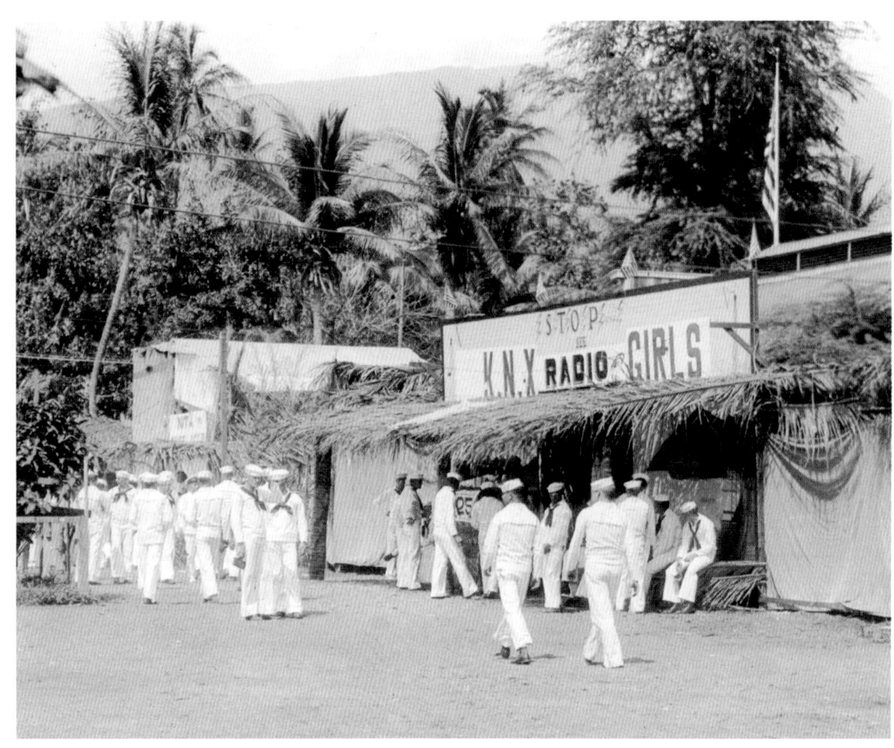
STOP
K.N.X RADIO GIRLS

Situated in the middle of the Pacific Ocean, the Hawaiian Islands are a strategic port of call for ships of all nations. Since the late 1700s, they have served as an exotic way station for people who began to arrive in substantial numbers for both trade and military purposes. As the population grew and the harbor area in Honolulu developed, sailors were drawn there for its abundance of entertainment options. The Iwilei, or red-light district, provided pleasure for sailors for nearly 200 years and made it one of the premier destinations in the South Seas, rivaling other infamous ports of call such as Shanghai, Hankow, and Manila.

The first Chinese immigrants arrived in Honolulu in 1788, brought over as cheap labor for the sugar fields and plantations. By 1882 they numbered over 5,000, with 75 percent of them living in the area of downtown Honolulu known as Chinatown. In addition to restaurants and supply stores that catered to the shipping industry, a lively vice district had developed and was immediately appropriated by sailors who absorbed all that Chinatown had to offer, including gambling dens, tattoo parlors, billiard halls, and bars.

The United States took possession of the islands in 1898 and made a concerted effort to market the Territory of Hawaii as an exotic tourist destination. Travel brochures and magazine advertisements flashed colorful imagery to portray Hawaii as a tropical Paradise filled with beautiful beaches, nubile hula girls, and powerful native surfers.

This imagery was also used in recruitment material for the U.S. Navy as an inducement to "see the World" while serving one's country. Descriptions of Chinatown's vice district were absent from materials marketed to tourists, but through popular lore and word of mouth sailors knew exactly where to go.

The buildup of U.S. military personnel after the attack on Pearl Harbor brought Honolulu into focus as the main debarkation point for thousands of sailors bound for the Pacific theater. According to a 1940 *Bluejacket's Manual*, liberty, aka shore leave, was granted by watches, with each watch alternating liberty on weekdays and 48-hour liberties on weekends. Before leaving ship, liberty parties were inspected by the officer of the deck. Soiled uniforms, un-shined shoes, and unkempt hair were considered grounds for not leaving the ship.

Loaded onto skiffs and dropped off in Honolulu, Navy personnel were deposited in front of the Army and Navy YMCA. Young and naïve, most sailors' perceptions of Hawaii as a tropical Paradise quickly deflated upon their arrival. Visions of a moonlit Diamond Head, available hula girls, and free-flowing and affordable rum dissolved into crowded streets, beaches cordoned off with barbed wire, and endless lines to nowhere. Still, as with many ports of call, amusements were plentiful, and set against the warm trade winds, sailors took advantage of the momentary diversions on their last stop to hell.

The "Y" served as a home away from home, directing servicemen to more wholesome types of activities. Organized sports, free coffee and donuts, and USO-sponsored dances were provided to boost their morale. But directly across the street from the YMCA was the immensely popular Black Cat Café. The draw at the Black Cat was the inexpensive food—10-cent hot dogs and 15-cent hamburgers—not to mention cheap booze and the usual gimmicks to entice tourists, which included hula girl pictures (two for 75 cents) and waste-your-nickel slot machines. Cheap pitchers of Royal beer and pineapple whisky shots meant the Black Cat was usually the first and last stop ashore.

Adjacent to the Black Cat, the area surrounding Hotel Street was a swarm of men roaming about aimlessly, looking for action or something to stimulate their abject boredom. Sidewalks were congested. One after another, bars such as Hoffman's, The Mint, and Two Jacks lured customers in. They advertised a four-drink minimum, usually served all at once and expected to be swigged down quickly before a bouncer asked you to move on. Restless servicemen also sought out taxi dancehalls where a dollar got you a strip of 10 tickets to dance with a girl. Every minute or so a bell rang and it was on to the next girl.

Along with pool halls, chow mein houses, and shoeshine peddlers was the inevitable line to get laid. With a nothing-to-lose attitude and the prospect of death looming just over the horizon, many young men wanted to have sex. The Rex, The Bronx, The New Senator, and about 10 other brothels operated in and around Hotel Street in Chinatown. Typically a customer waited in line on the sidewalk for up to an hour. Sometimes, to boost their libido, they arrived drunk, though if they were too drunk they were not allowed entrance. Once inside, a choice was made of which woman to go with. When that was determined, sometimes by sight, sometimes by recommendation, there was another short wait on a bench. When it was time, the customer was hustled into a pared-down room consisting of a cot, a wash basin, and an alarm clock. More often than not first-time customers came just by being touched, while the more experienced who tried to prolong the act were hustled out, finished or not, once the alarm went off. The entire experience lasted

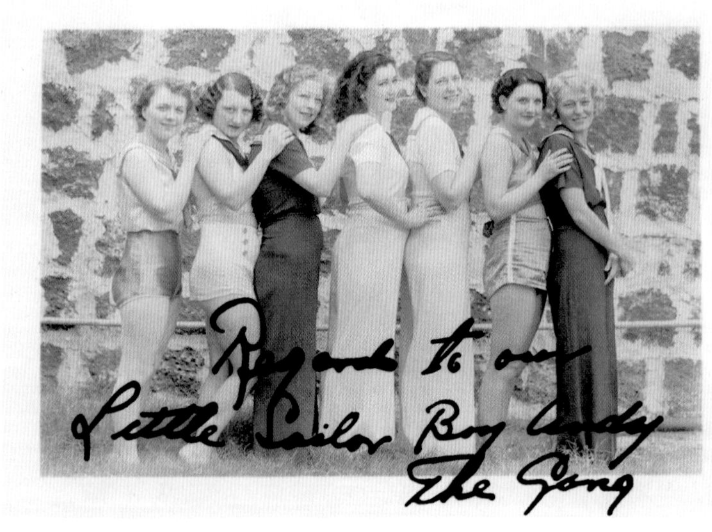
Regards to our
Little Sailor Boy Andy
The Gang

three minutes. To speed things up, oral sex was sometimes substituted for intercourse, which many customers thoroughly enjoyed. Outside, first-timers were greeted by friends, and a celebratory tattoo was in order. Conveniently located on Hotel Street were at least eight tattoo parlors, including the famed Sailor Jerry whose shop was next to Hoffman's bar.

When carousing Chinatown grew stale some of the more adventurous servicemen would pool their resources, grab a car, and become unabashed sightseeing tourists. The Pali, the Punch Bowl, and the Dole pineapple plant were popular destinations for restless swabbies. Closer to base was the popular Pearl City Tavern. There, a "monkey bar" featured an assortment of live monkeys that would throw their feces when provoked by beer-swigging sailors. Walking on top of the bar, another monkey might solicit change with a tin cup. Noncompliance resulted in having your drink knocked over. But what many sailors went there for was a chance to throw a few punches at Marines.

Kau Kau Korner, a drive-in restaurant at the border of Waikiki, was a favored photo opportunity along with the Aloha Tower and the statue of King Kamehameha near the Iolani Palace. Waikiki afforded some entertainment but was tame compared to Chinatown. The Waikiki Tavern was one of a few bars frequented by sailors, and the Waikiki Theater, like all movie theaters in Honolulu, was packed with servicemen. P.Y. Chong's Lau Yee Chai restaurant made the list of must-see places, though slightly over budget for the average enlisted man. The two main Waikiki attractions, The Moana and Royal Hawaiian hotels, had been altered to accommodate the war. The Moana remained a guest hotel serving mostly military personnel while the Royal Hawaiian was reserved for sailors on a 10-day R&R. Hula lessons and more refined activities were meant to distract the troops, but ultimately most roads led back to Chinatown.

By 1944, as the fear of a Japanese invasion subsided, Hawaii seemed to relax. When martial law was eliminated in the summer of that year, civilian police resumed control of the vice district. The local government saw as one of its first tasks to eliminate the brothels. Chinatown continued to offer servicemen the assorted distractions that had defined it throughout the war years, but getting laid was no longer one of them.

When Japan surrendered in 1945, Honolulu's military presence quickly faded. For locals, military fatigue had set in. Wave after wave of servicemen had taken their toll, and the predictability of their antics while on shore leave had left mild resentment among native Hawaiians. The image of sailors lining the sidewalks receded to a distant memory as tourism became one of the prime economic generators for Honolulu. Chinatown, though rid of its brothels, continued to attract sailors looking for a good time. The remaining attractions—bars, pool halls, and tattoo parlors—continued to do modest business but never to the extent that propelled them during the war.

For the millions of sailors and soldiers who passed through Honolulu, shore leave had felt exotic and forbidden, but also banal and lonely. It was a time in which they were able to remove the war from their immediate reality and realize their manhood and youth, if only for a few hours, in a time that would never be again.

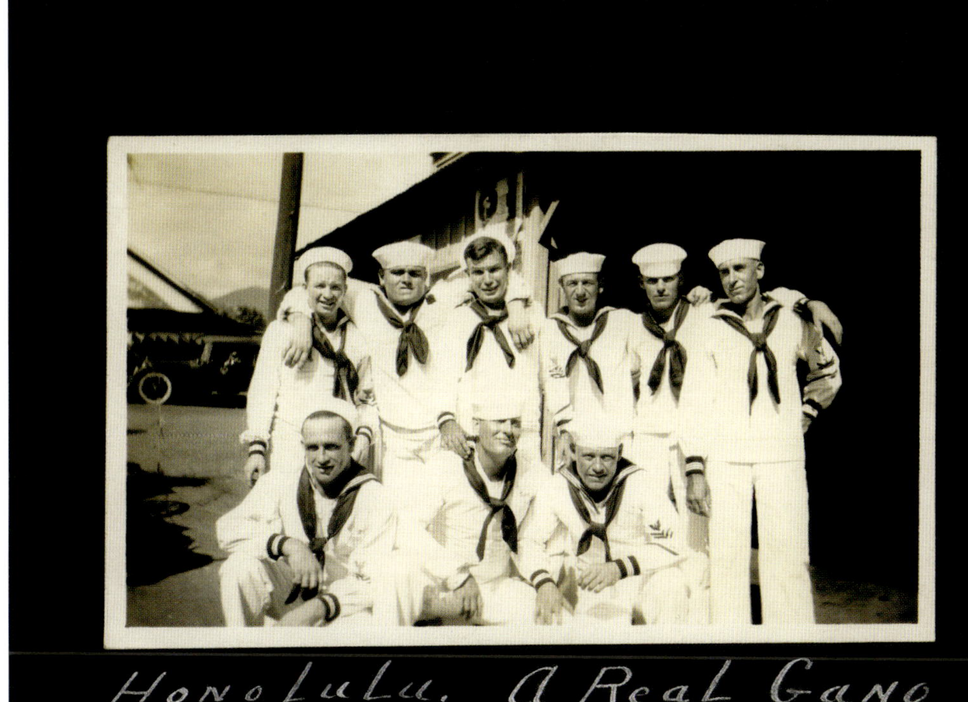

Honolulu. A Real Gangs
A Real Party.

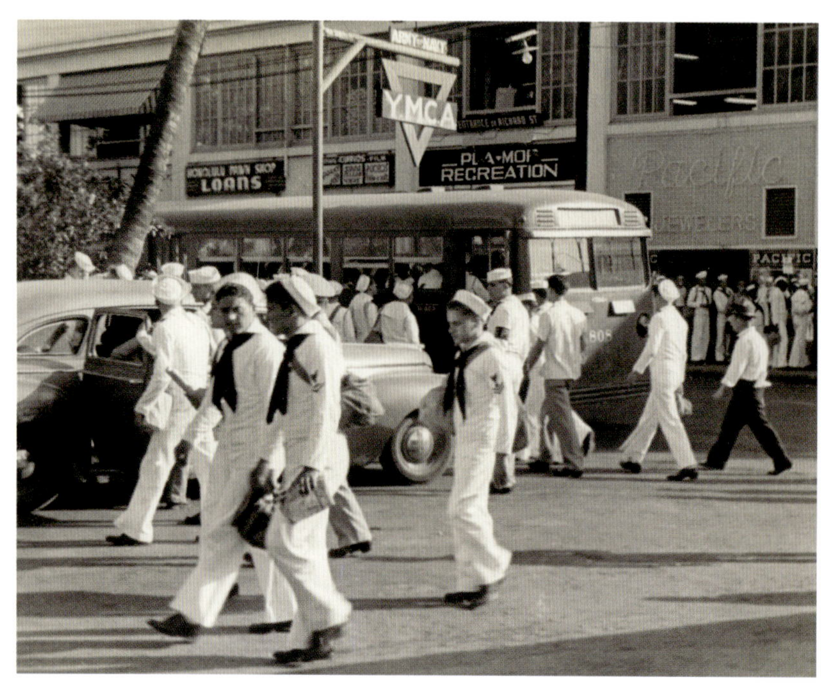

ARMY-NAVY
Y.M.C.A
LOANS
RECREATION
Pacific
JEWELERS
PACIFIC

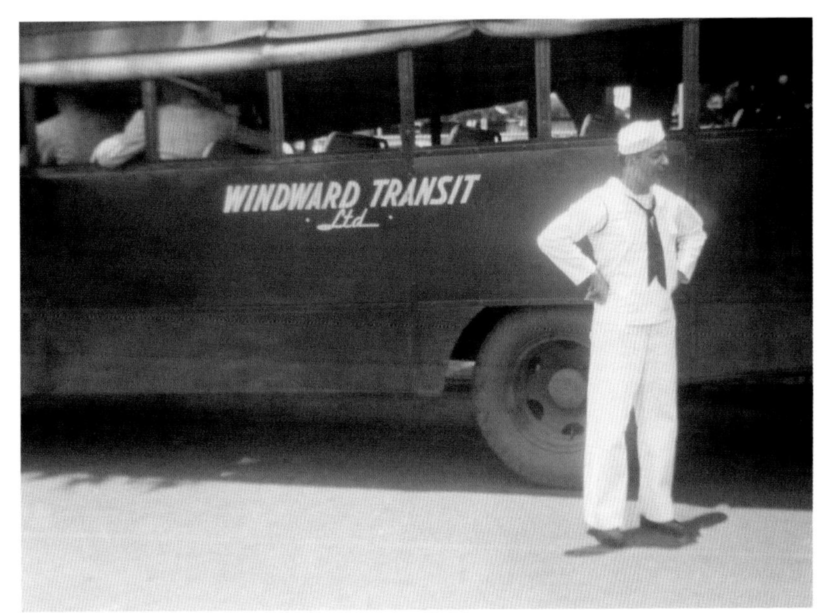
WINDWARD TRANSIT
Ltd

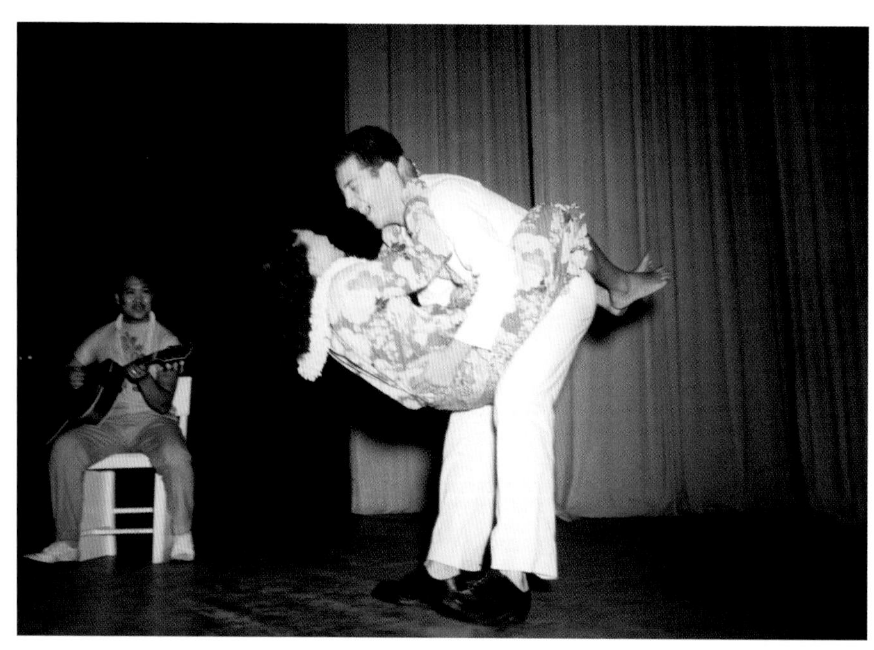

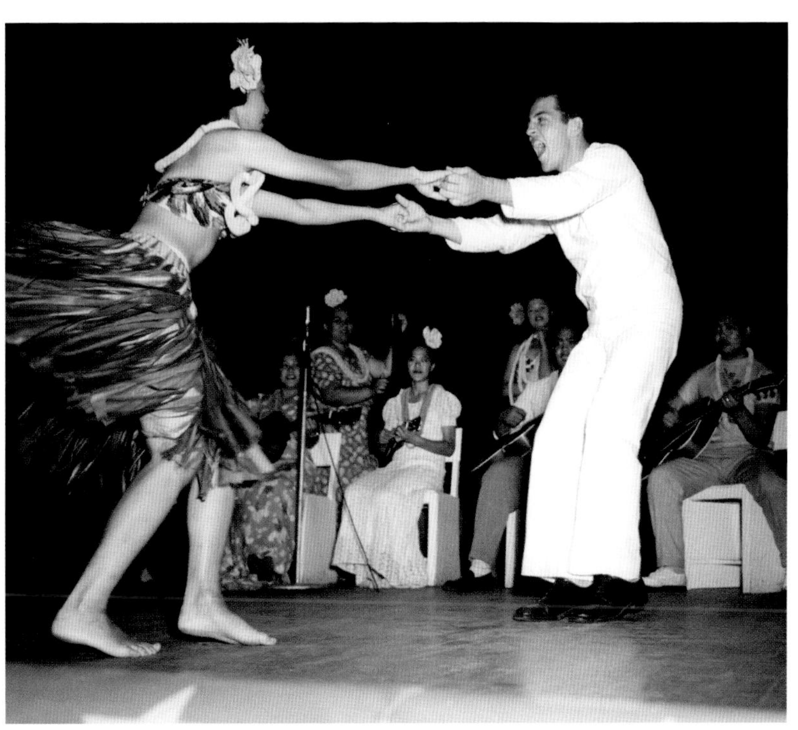

OLD'S TAXI

CARS STATIONED
KING AND RICHARDS STREETS
AND AT WAIKIKI

PHONE 2411

SPECIAL RATES FOR ISLAND TOURS

NO CHARGE FOR EXTRA PASSENGERS

NOTE: ALL NEW SEDANS
DRIVEN BY EXPERT HAOLE DRIVERS

PRESENTED BY Steve

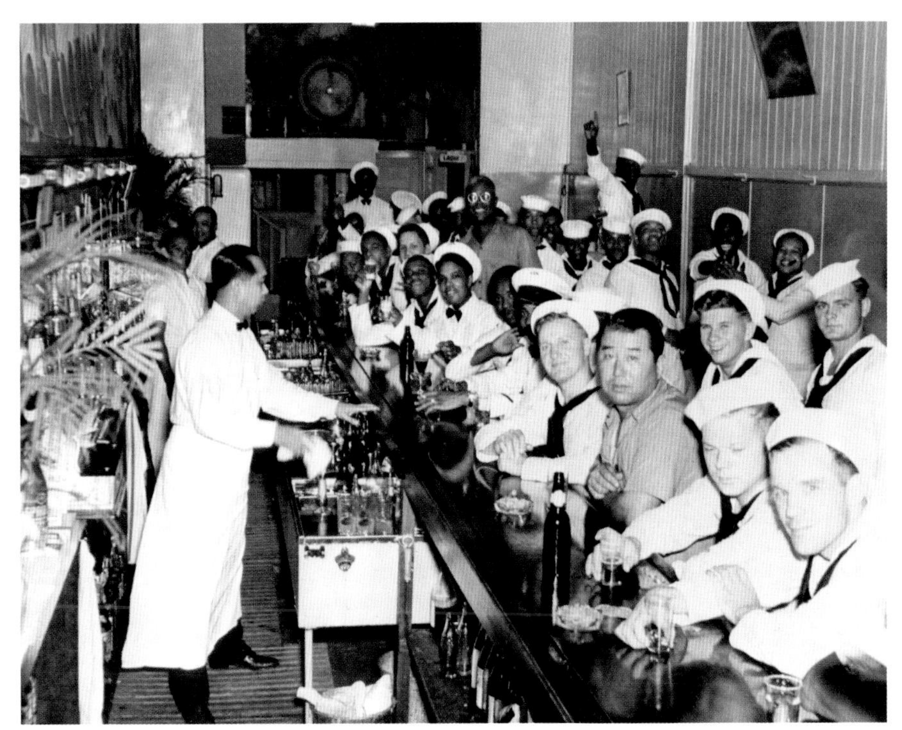

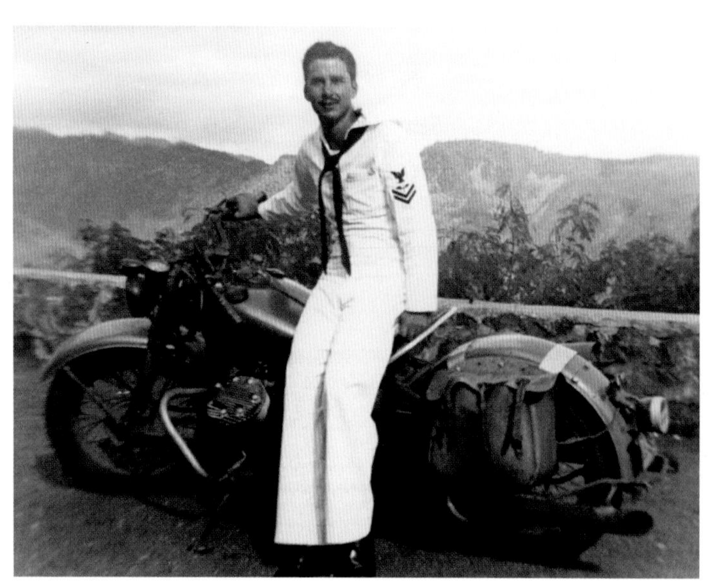

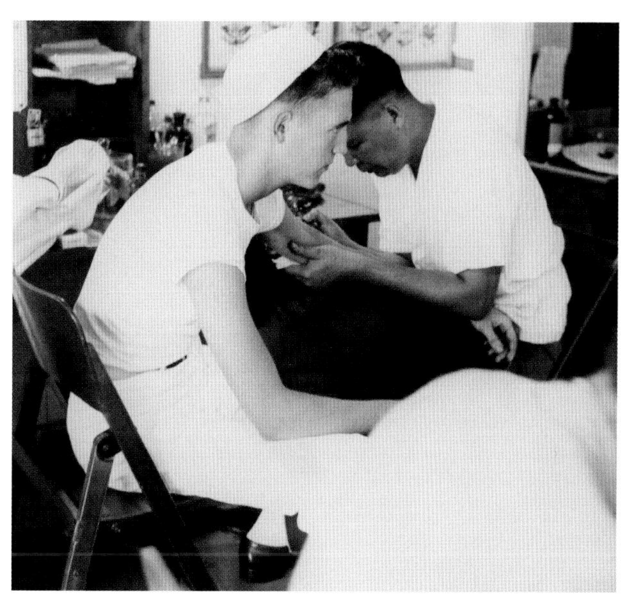

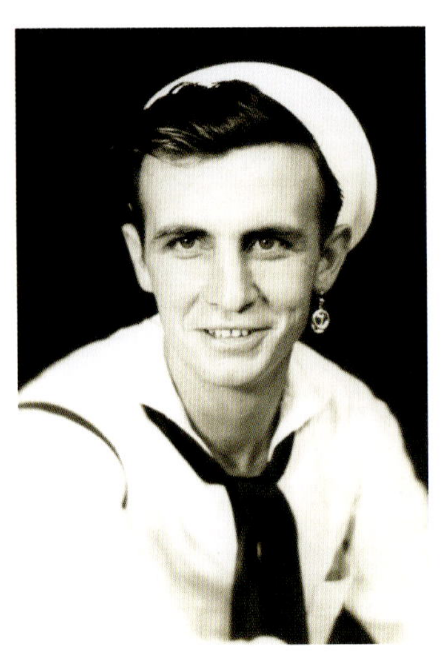

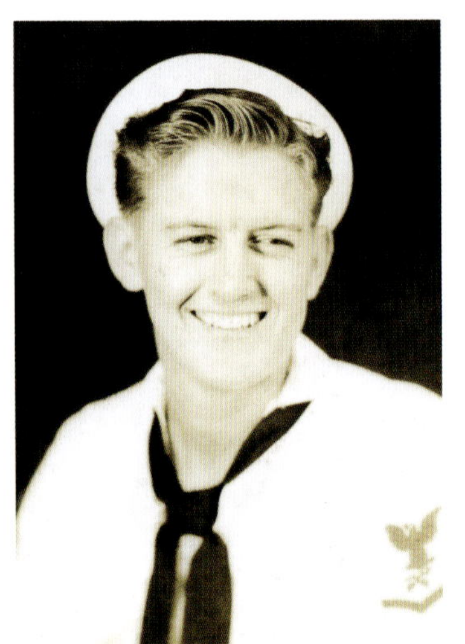

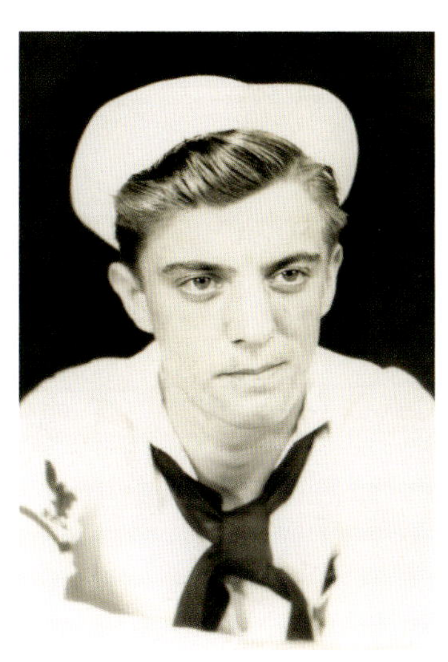

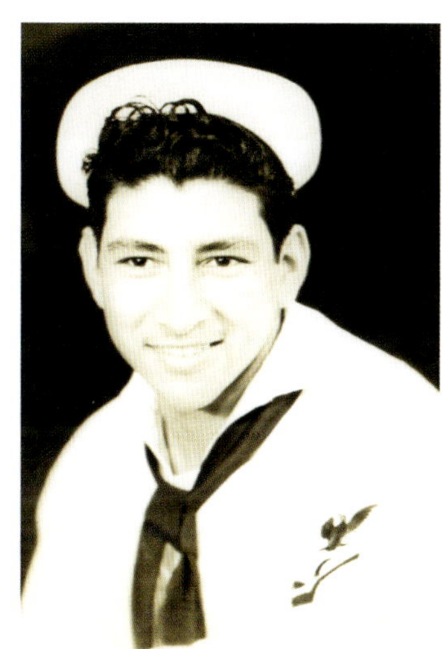

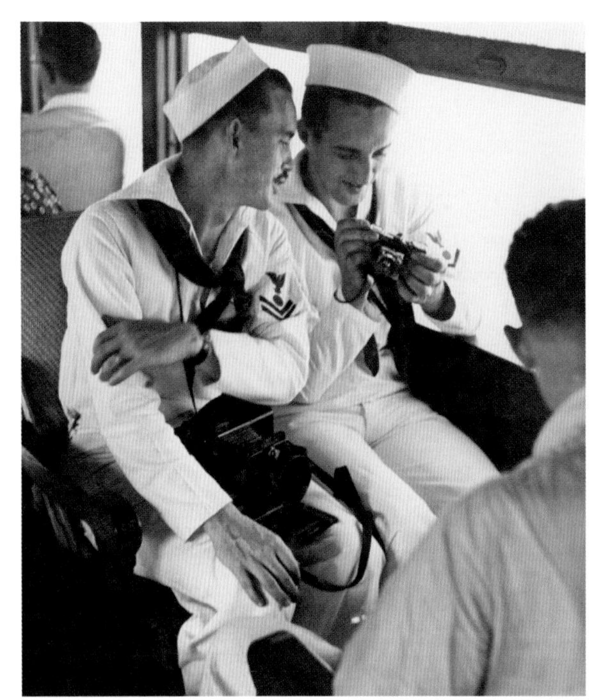

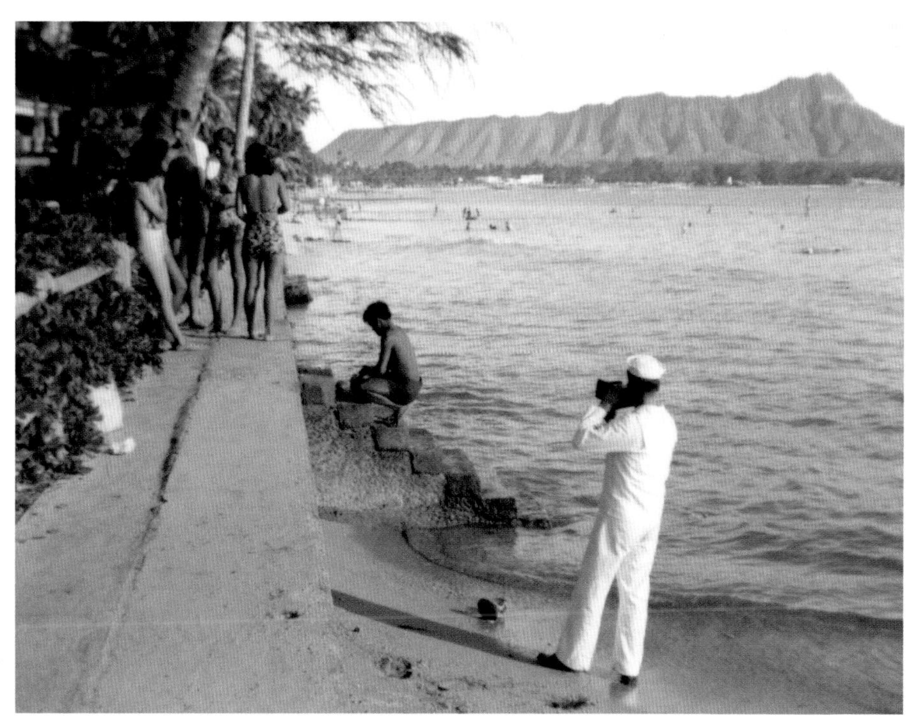

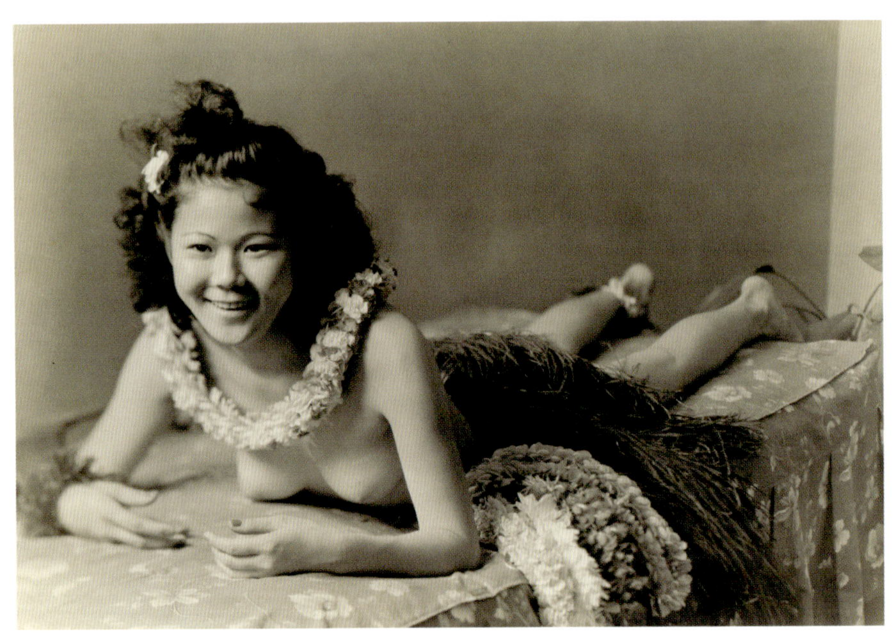

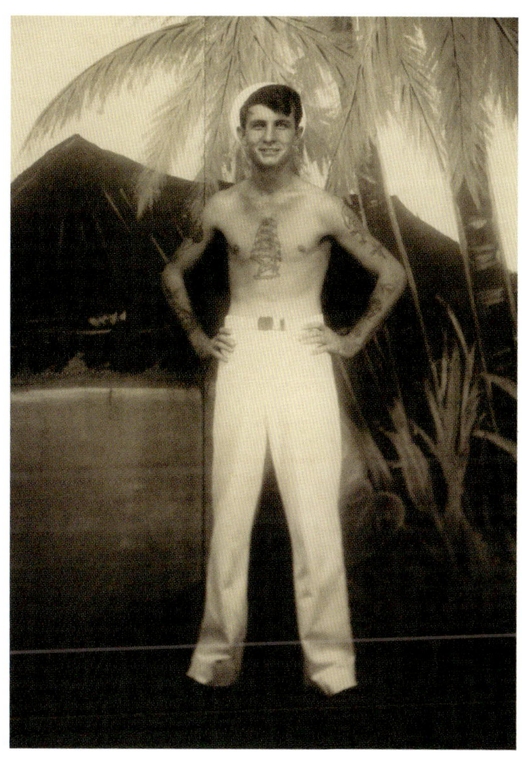

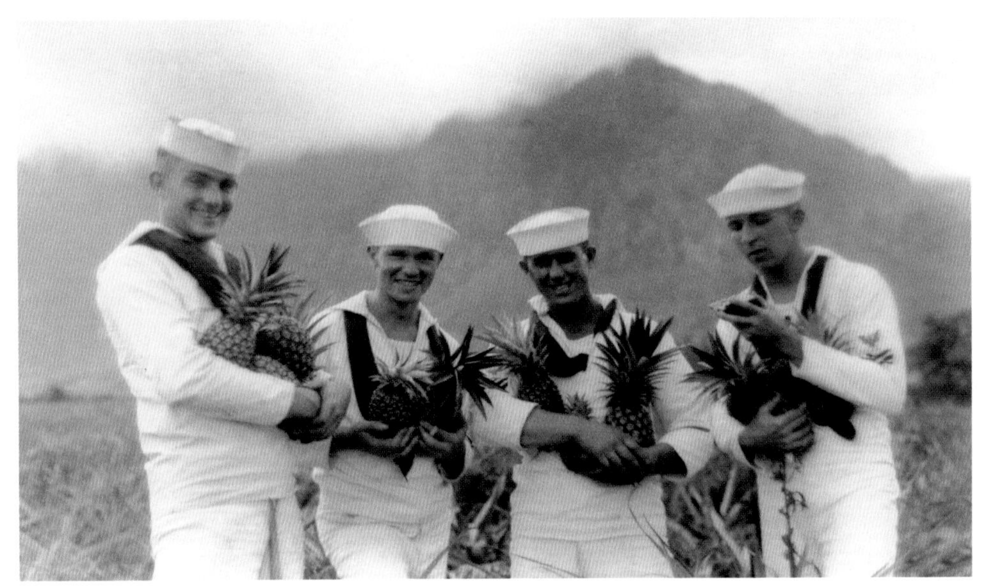

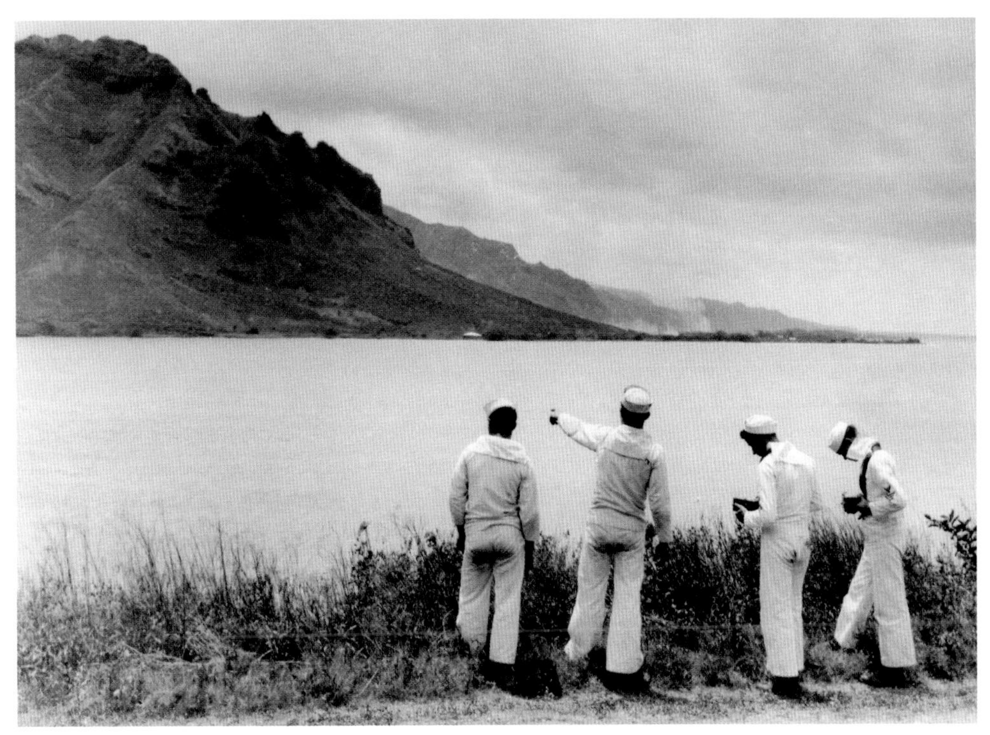

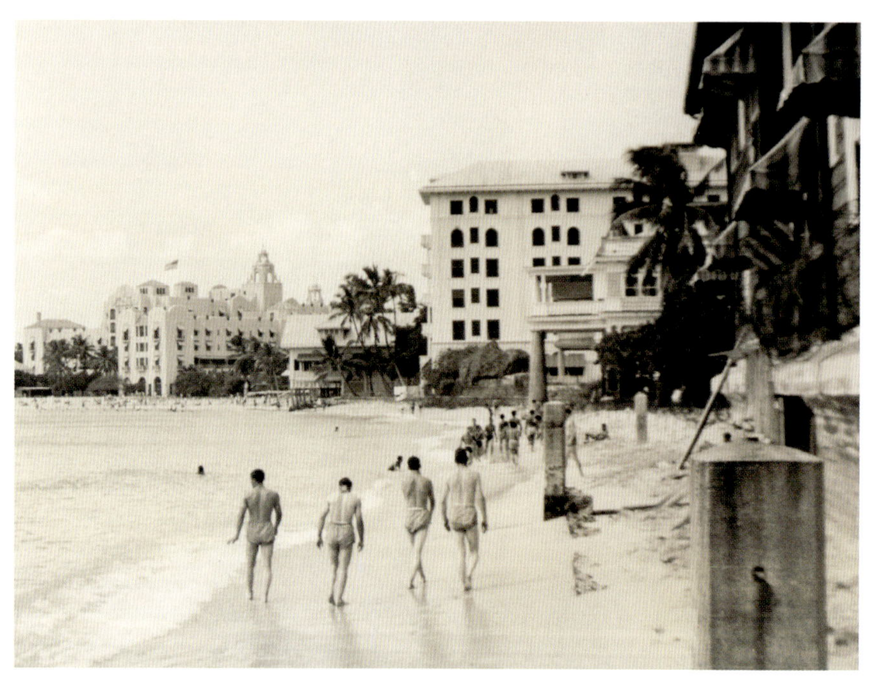

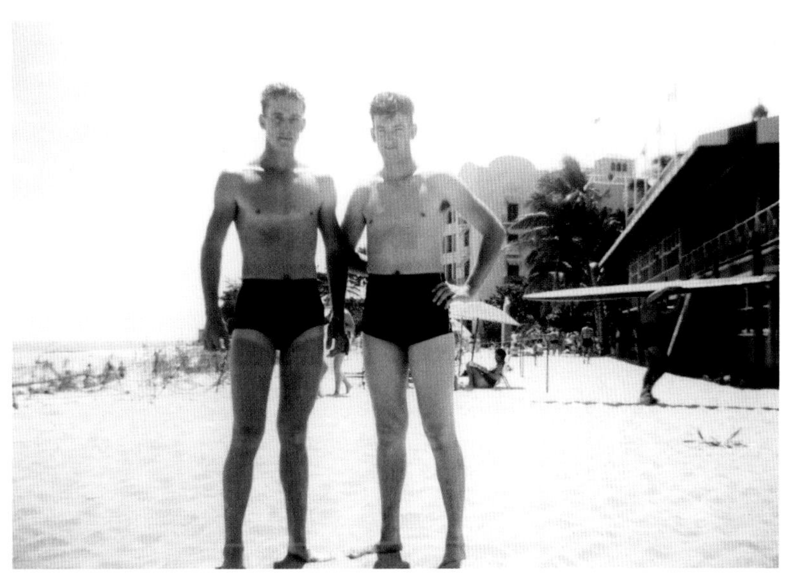

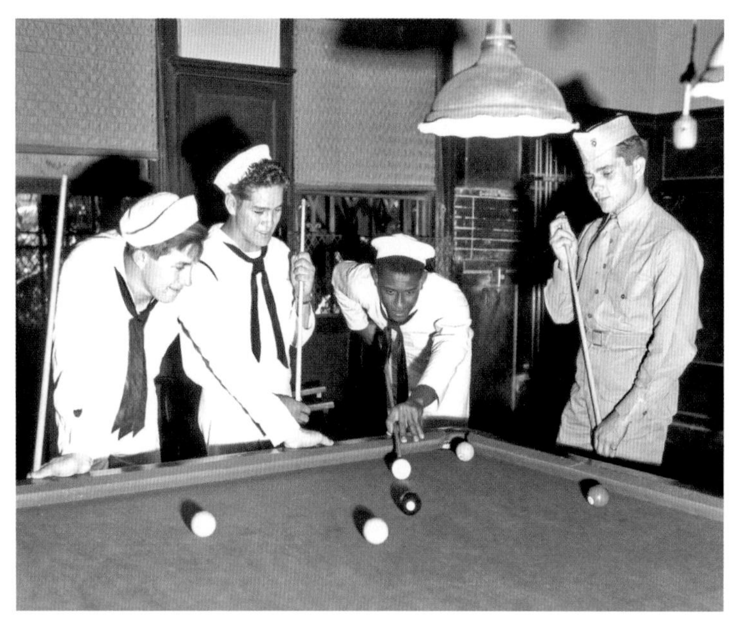

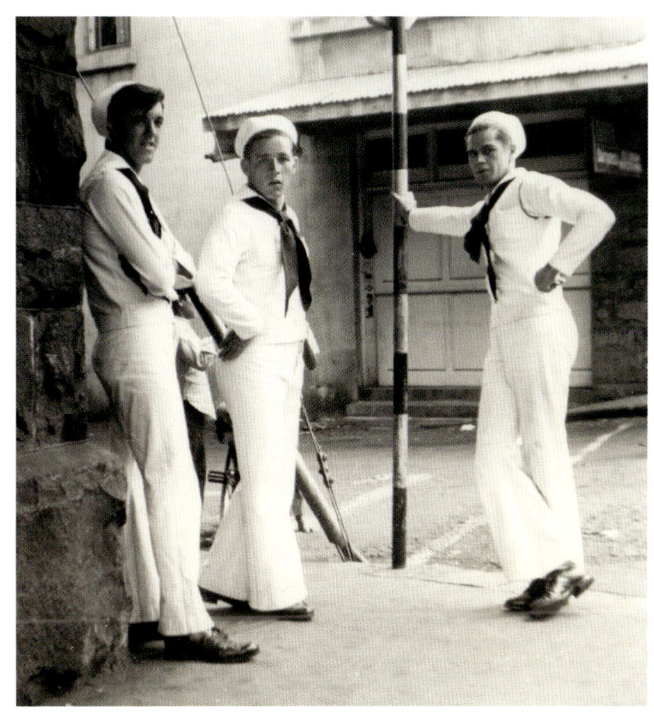

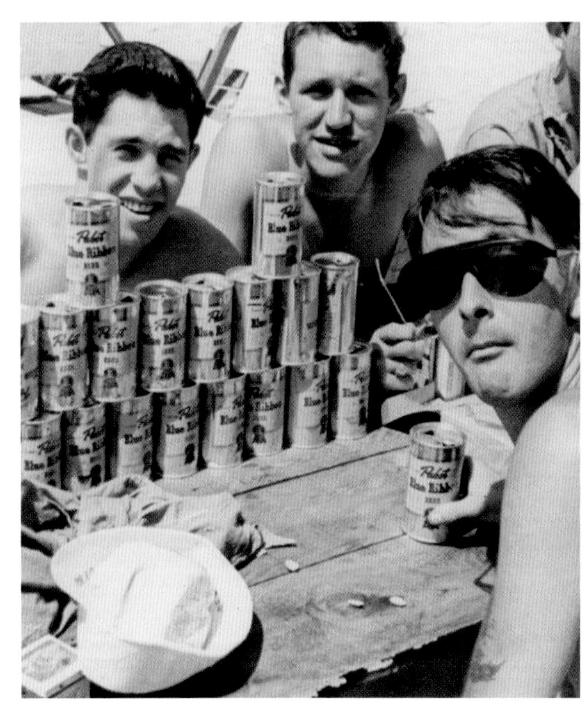

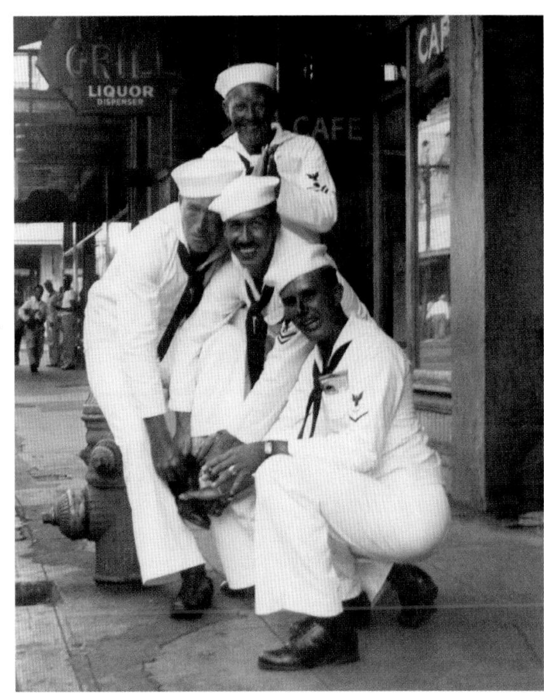
LIQUOR
CAFE

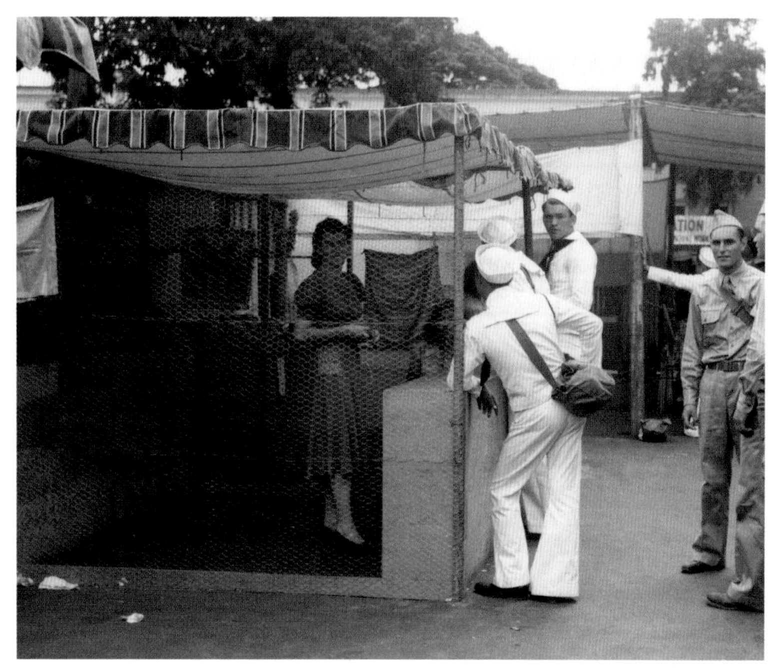

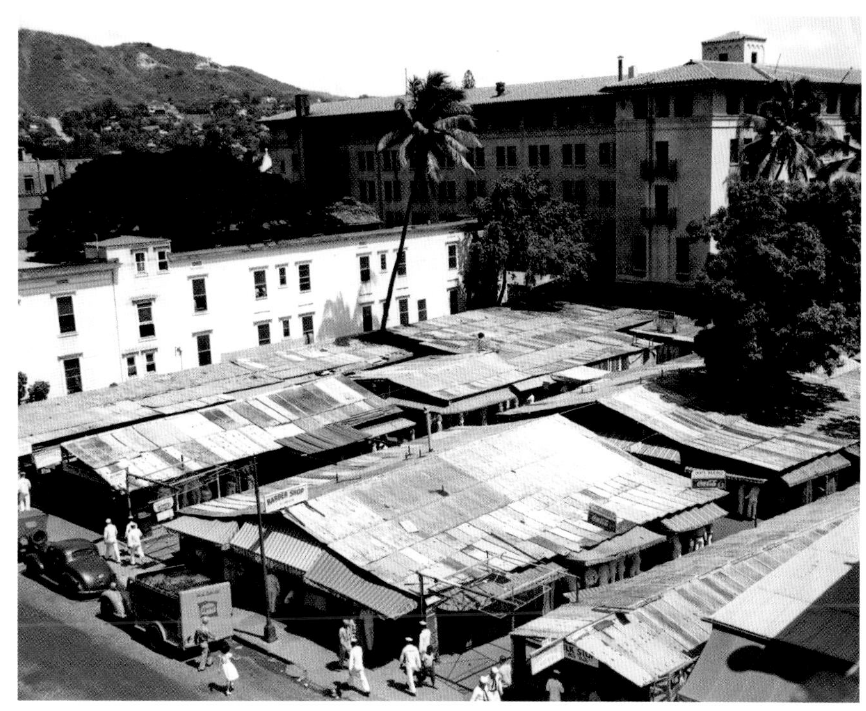
BARBER SHOP
Coca-Cola

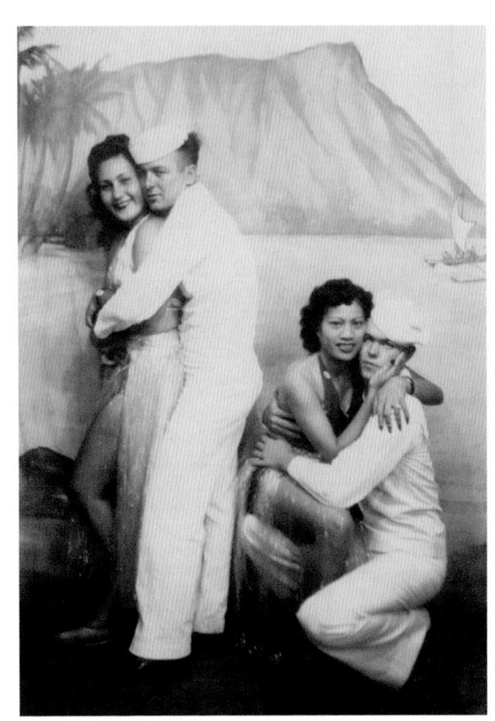

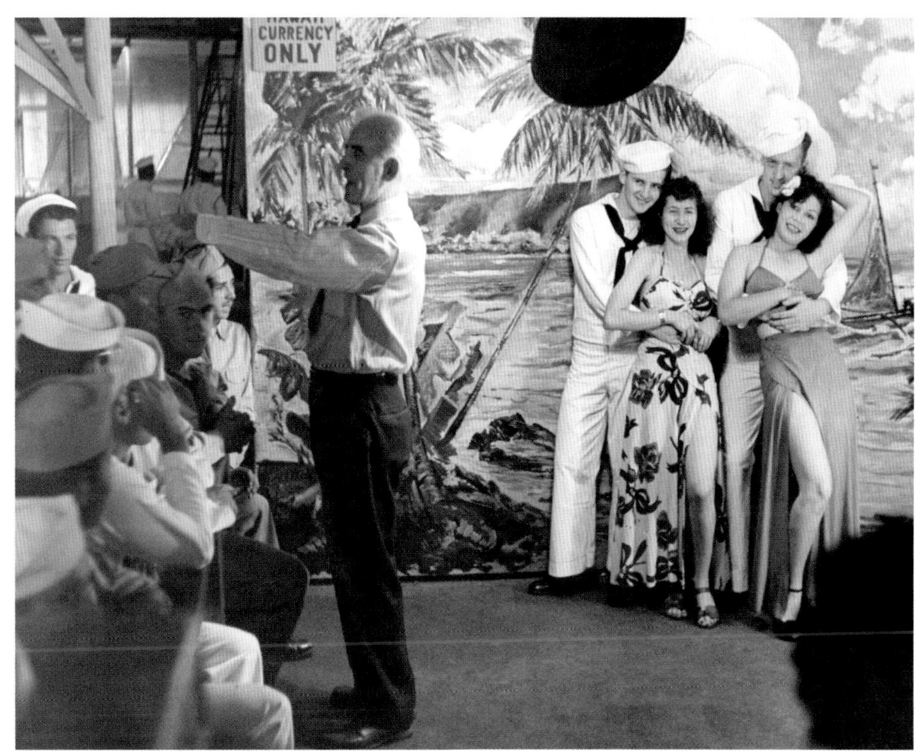
CURRENCY
ONLY

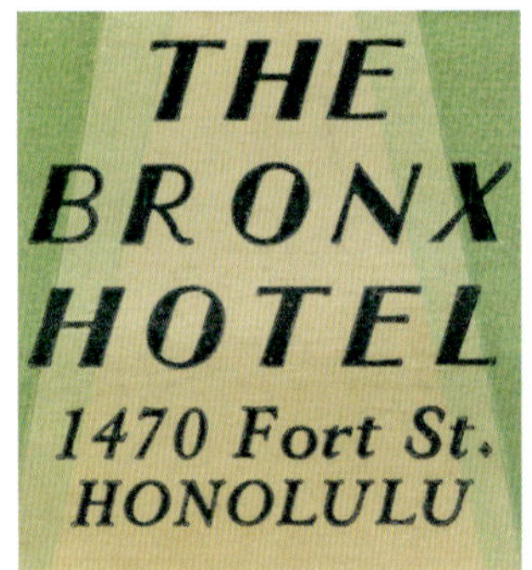
THE
BRONX
HOTEL
1470 Fort St.
HONOLULU

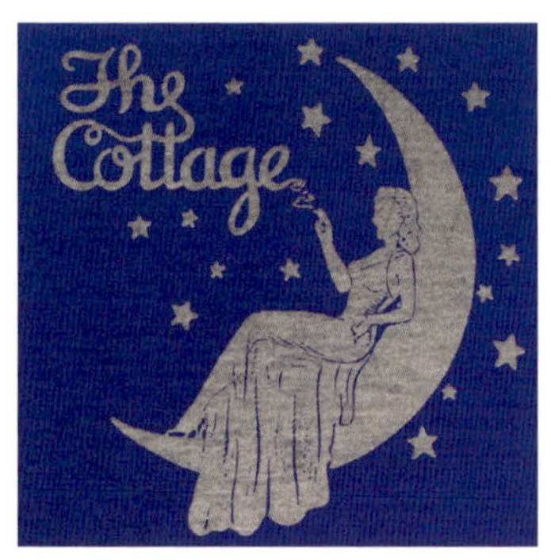
The
Cottage

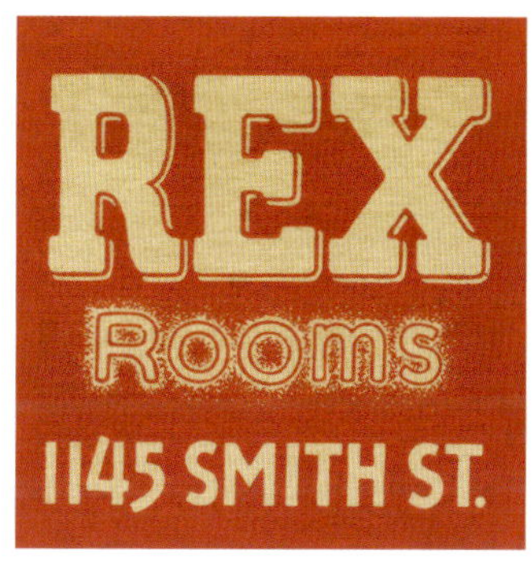
REX
Rooms
1145 SMITH ST.

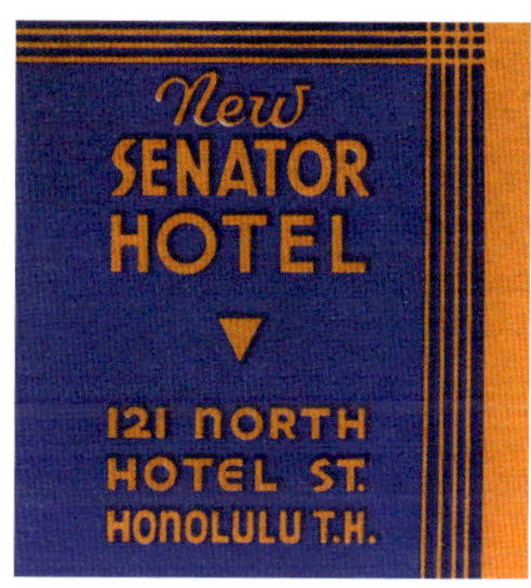
New
SENATOR
HOTEL
121 NORTH
HOTEL ST.
HONOLULU T.H.

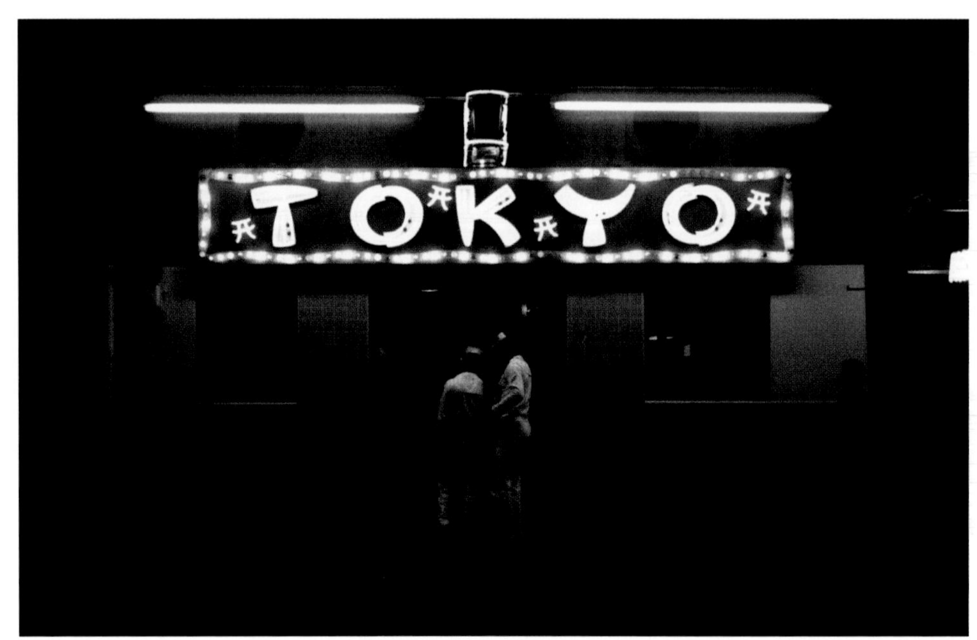
TOKYO

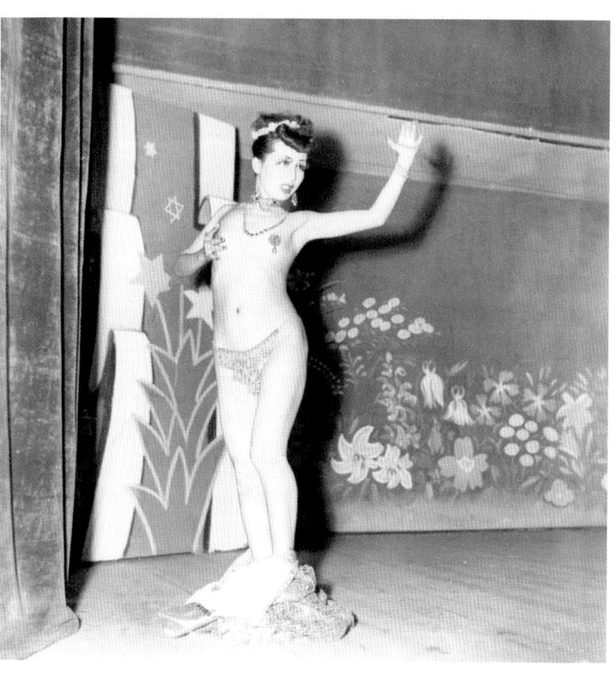

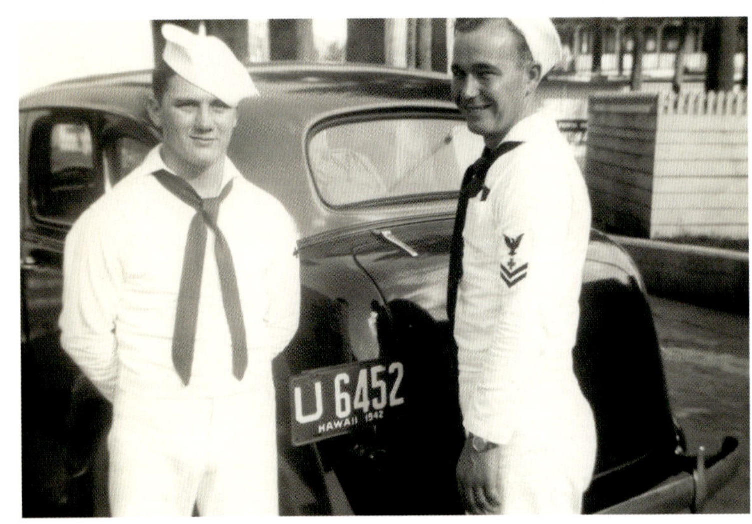
U 6452
HAWAII 1942

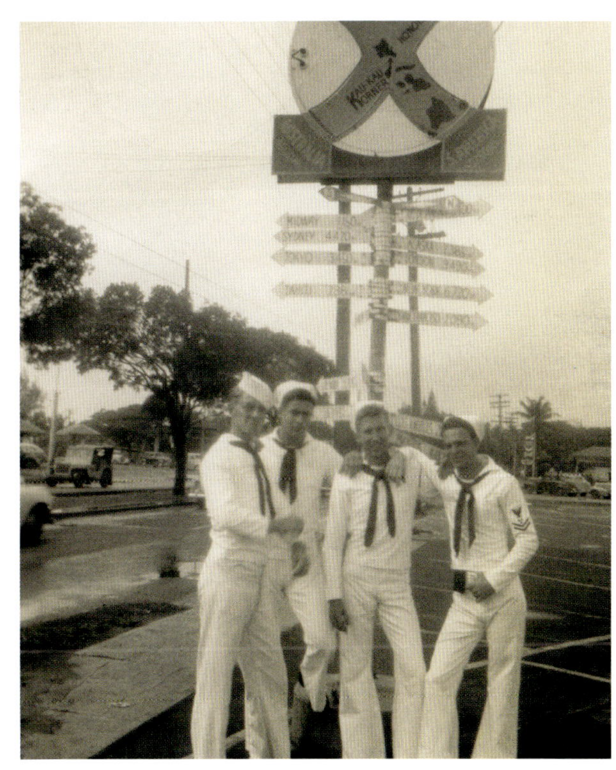

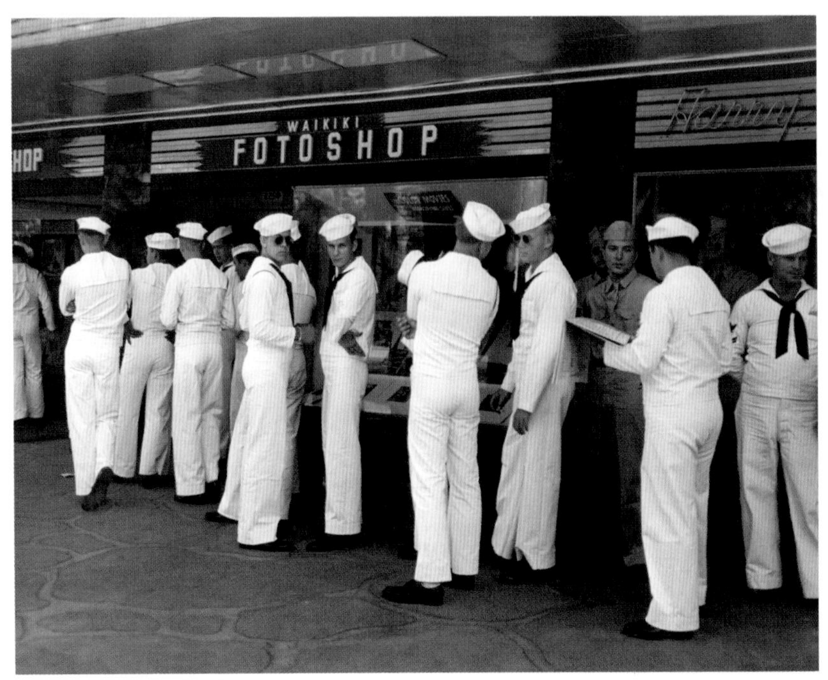
WAIKIKI
FOTOSHOP
HOP

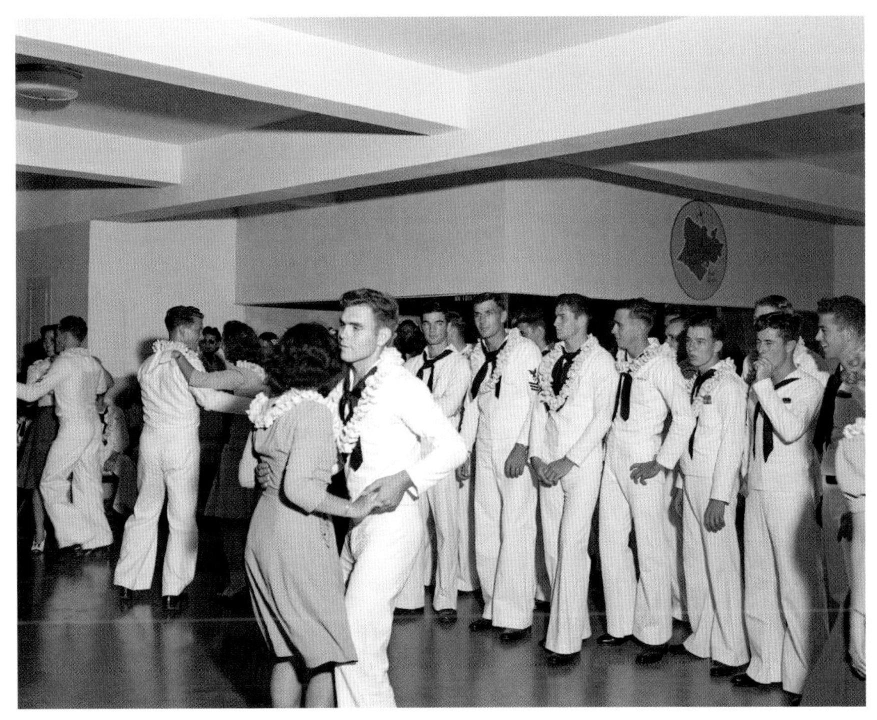

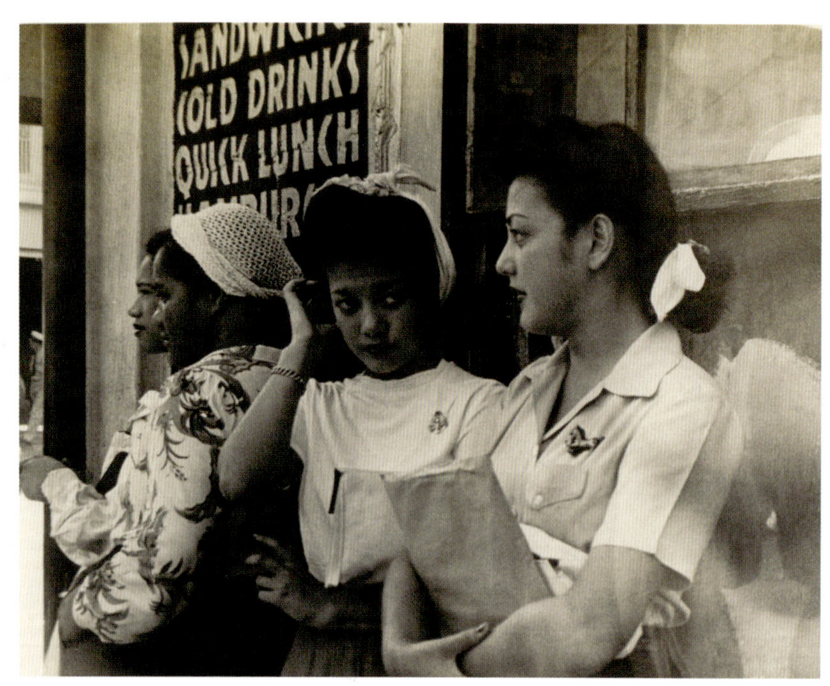
COLD DRINKS
QUICK LUNCH

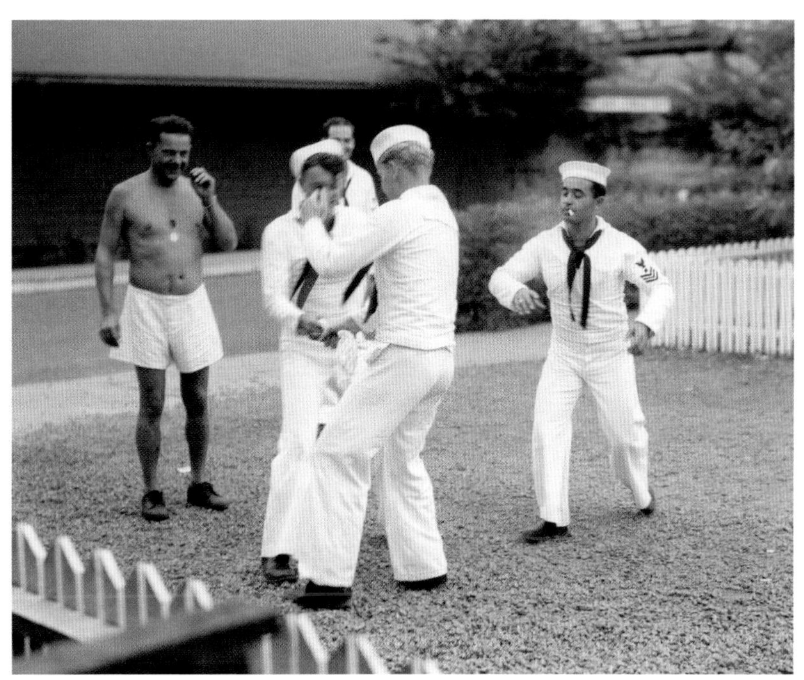

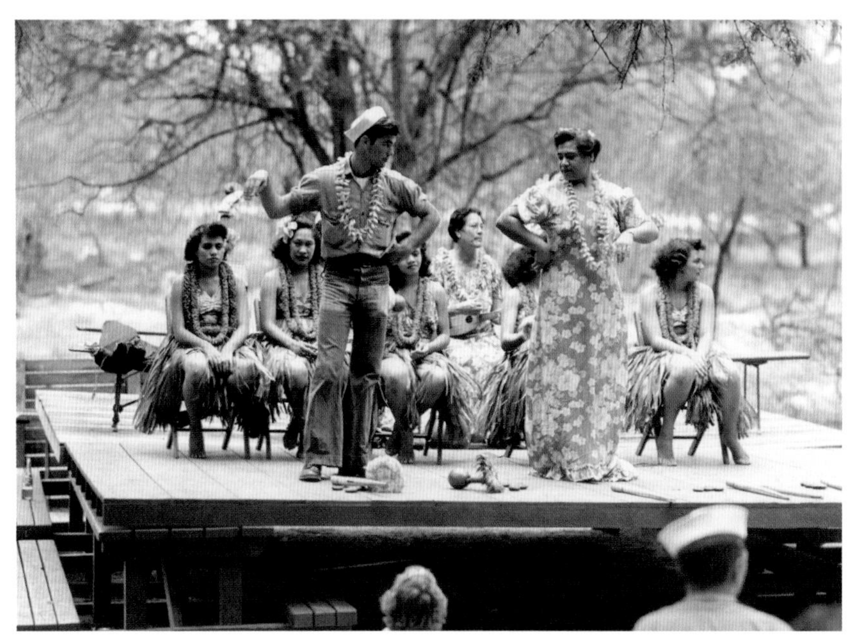

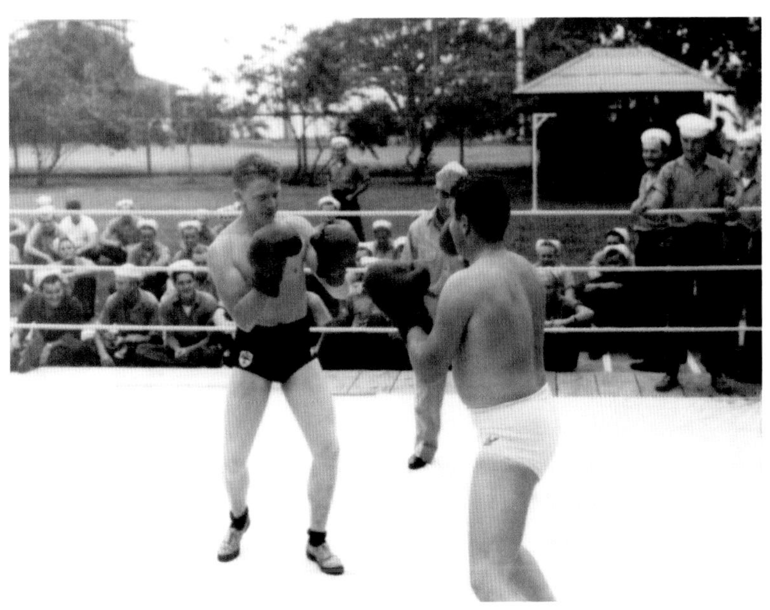

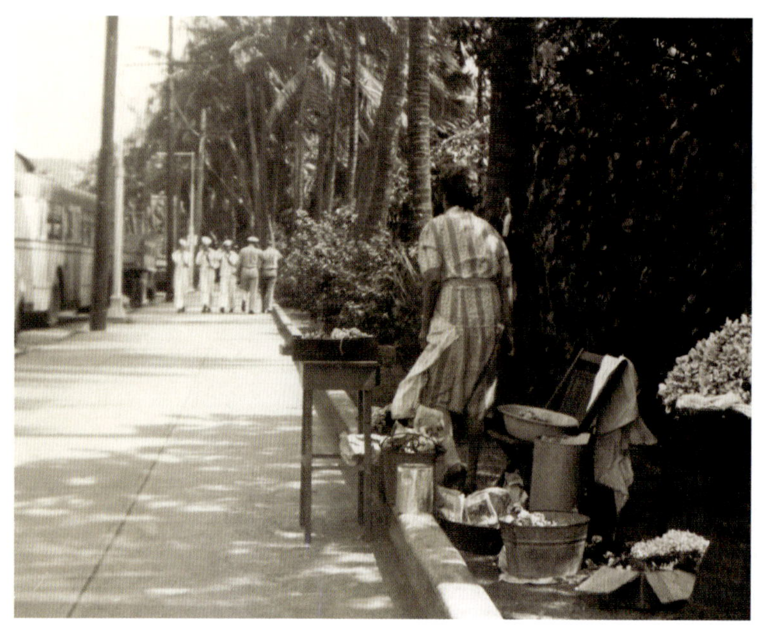

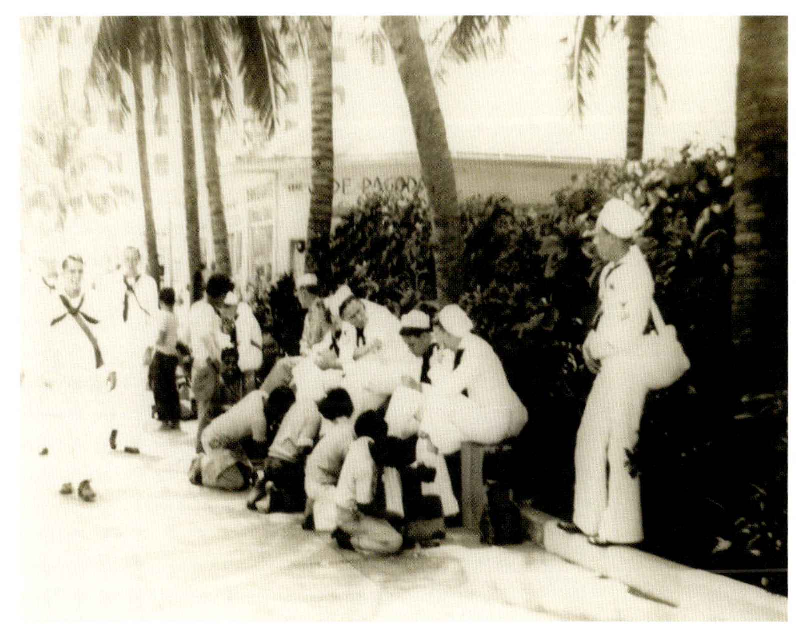

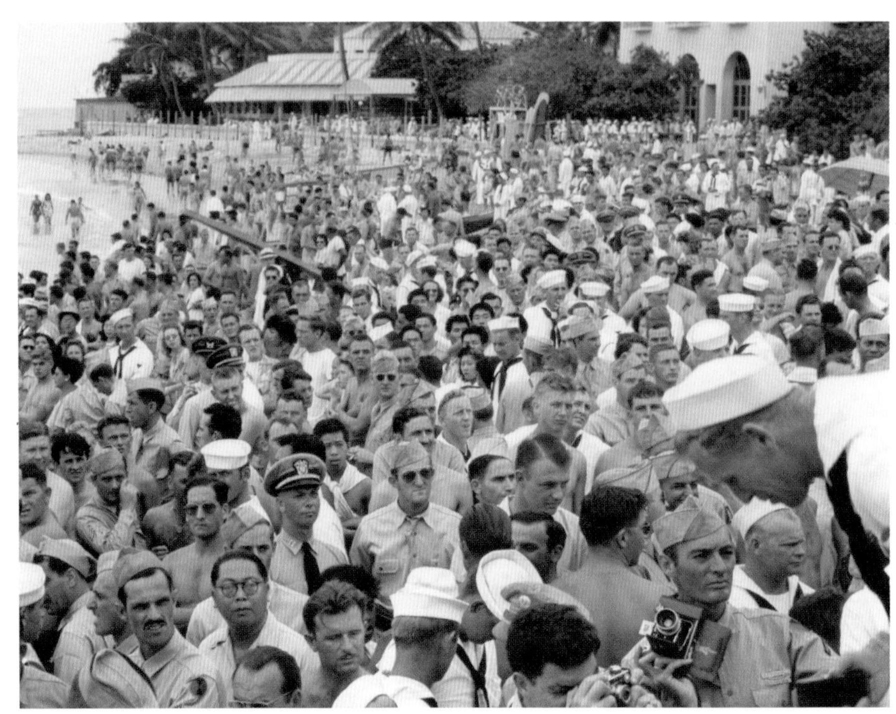

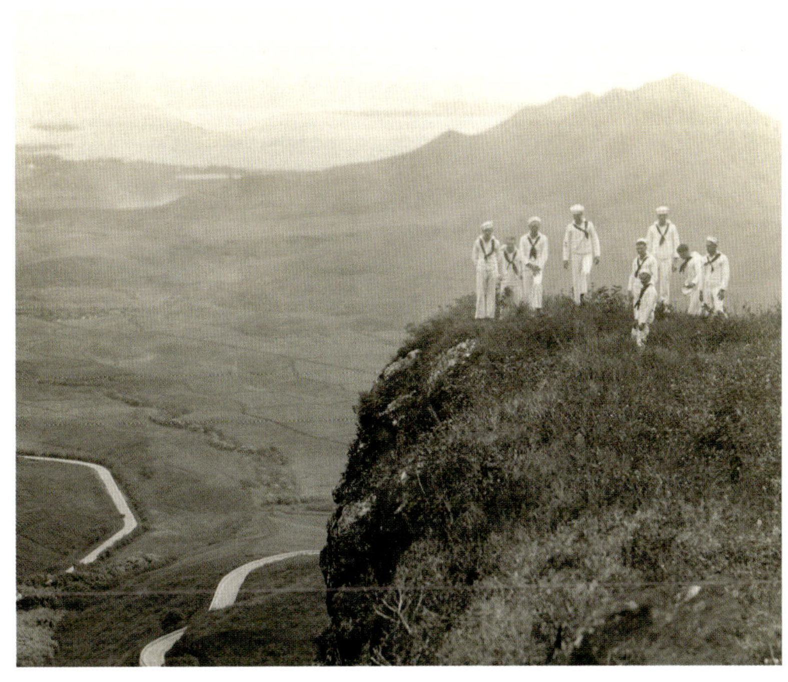

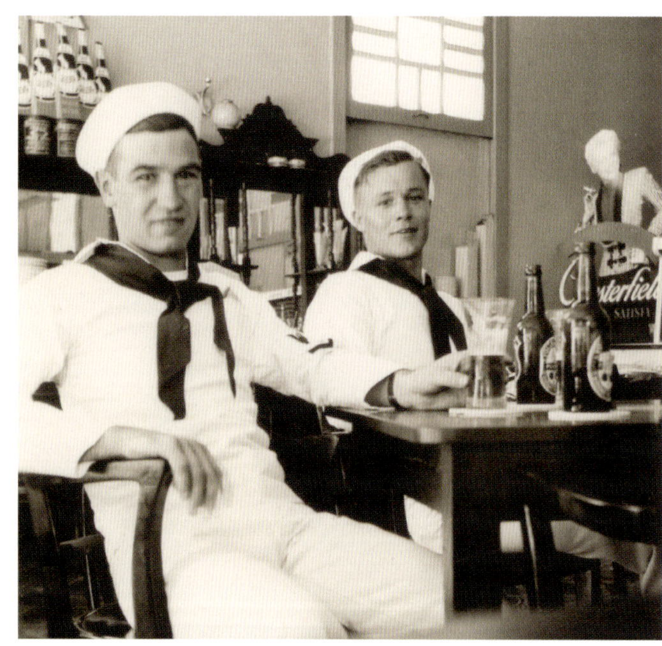

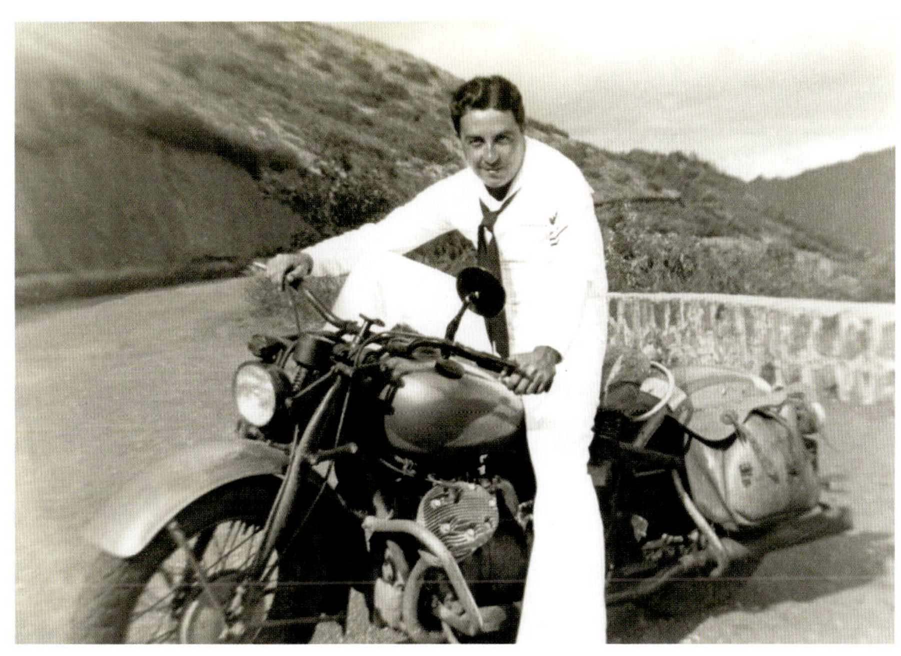

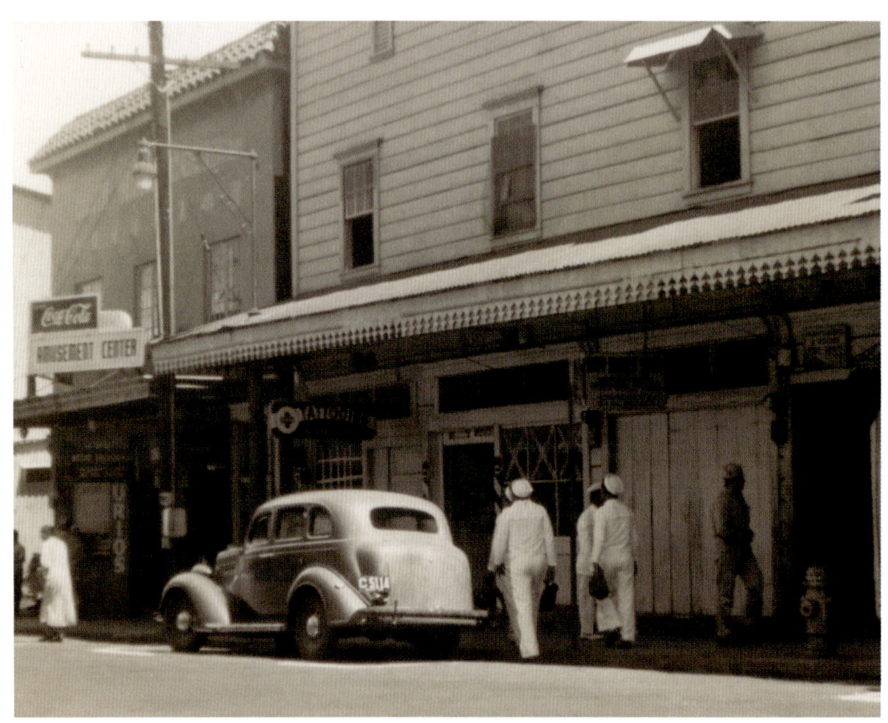
Coca-Cola
AMUSEMENT CENTER

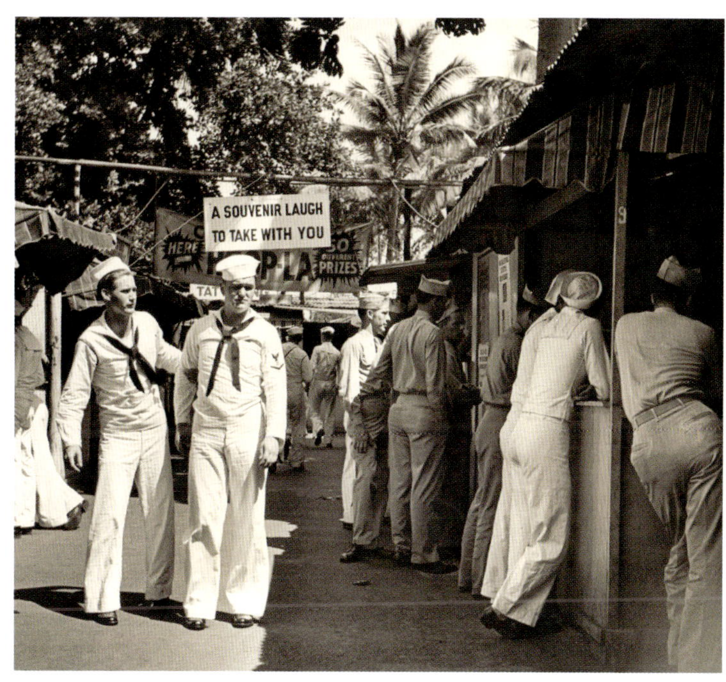
A SOUVENIR LAUGH
TO TAKE WITH YOU
HERE
PRIZES

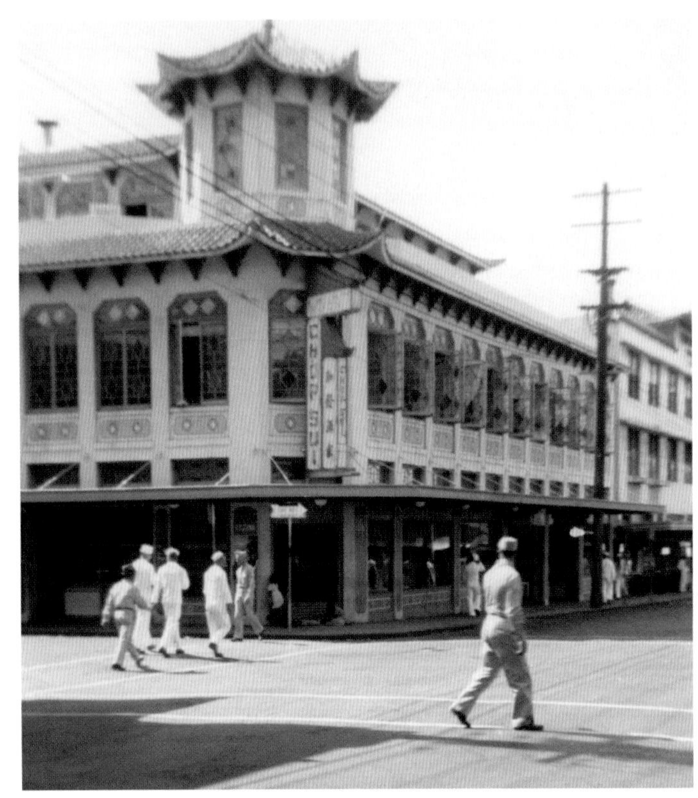

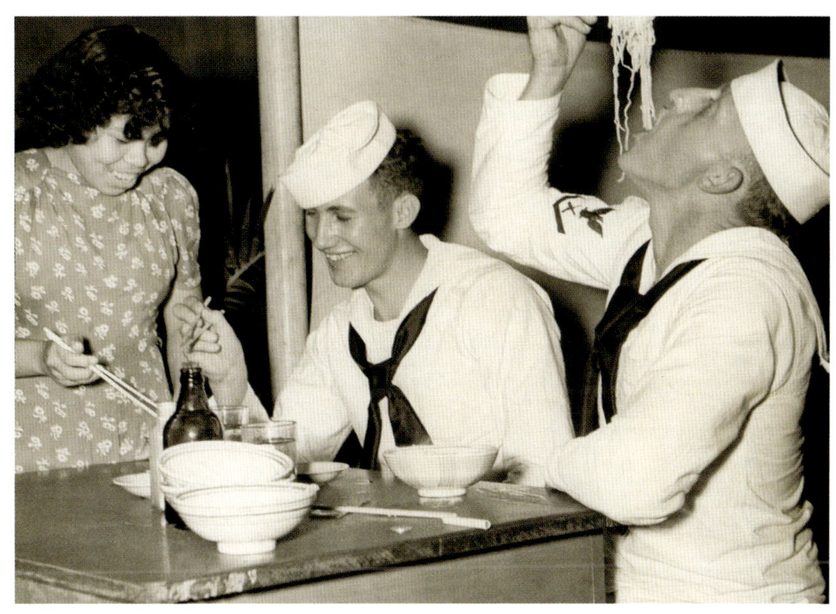

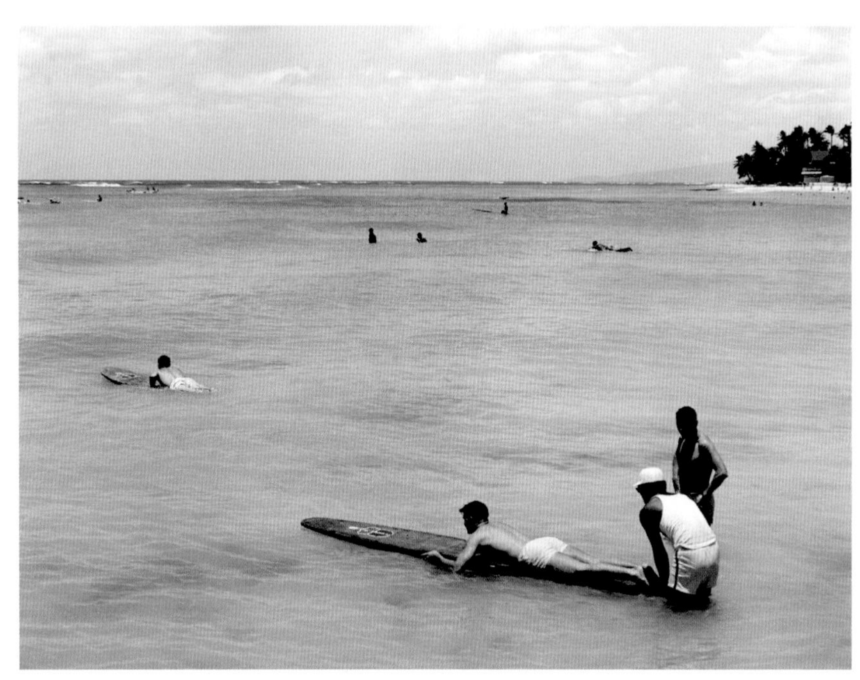

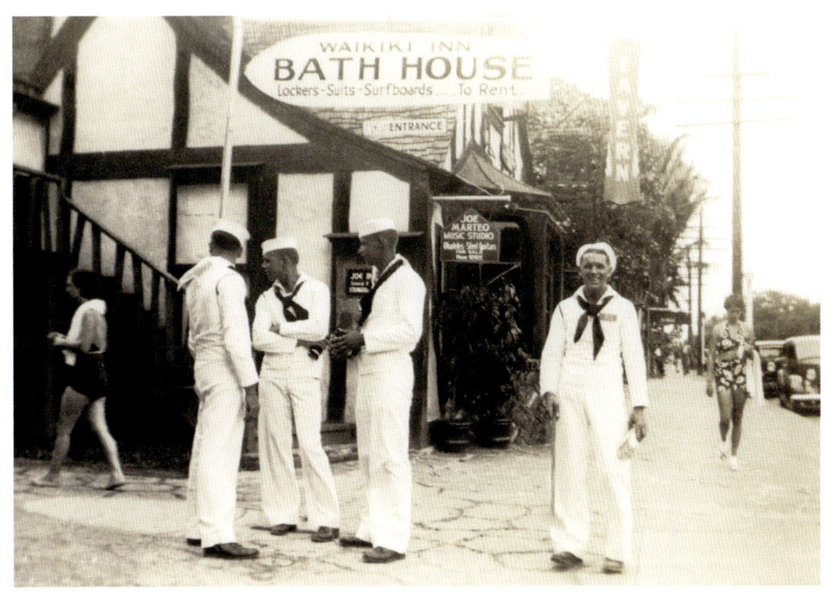
WAIKIKI INN
BATH HOUSE
Lockers - Suits - Surfboards ..... To Rent.
ENTRANCE
JOE
MARTEO
MUSIC STUDIO

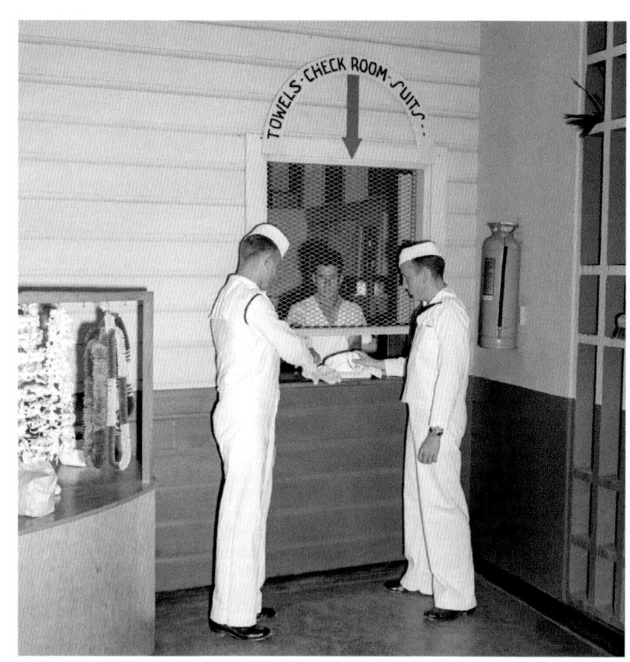
TOWELS · CHECK ROOM · SUITS

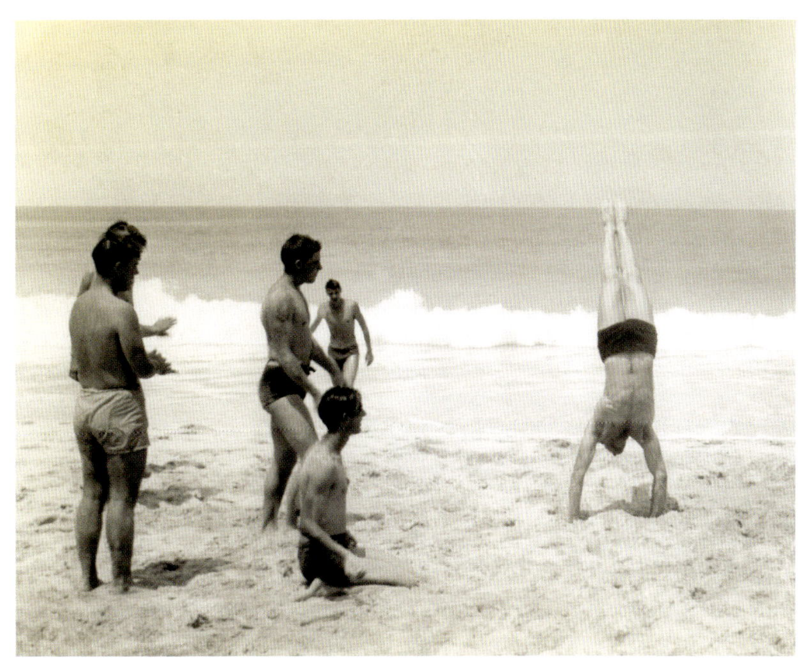

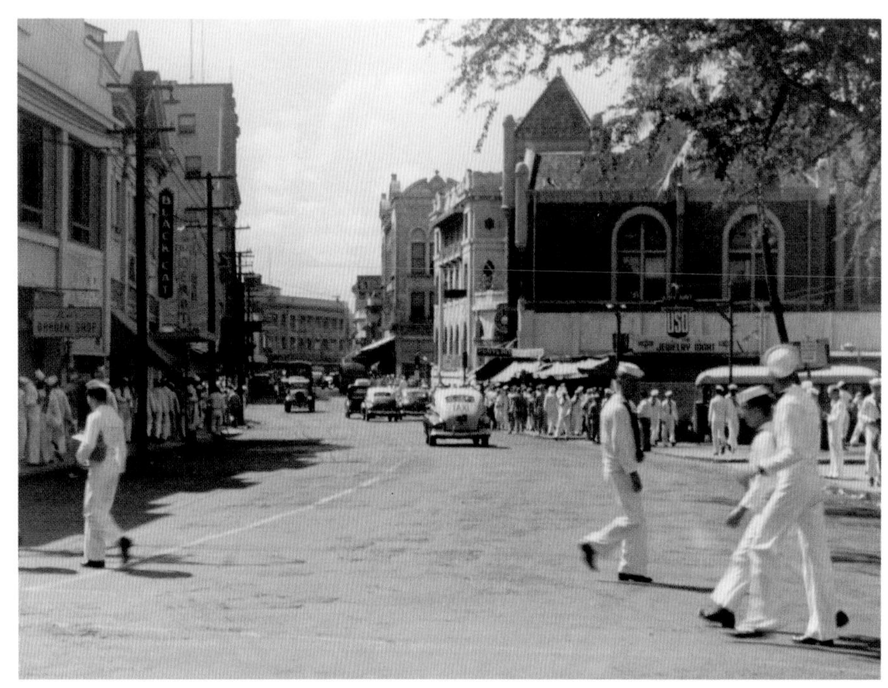
BLACK CAT
BARBER SHOP
USO

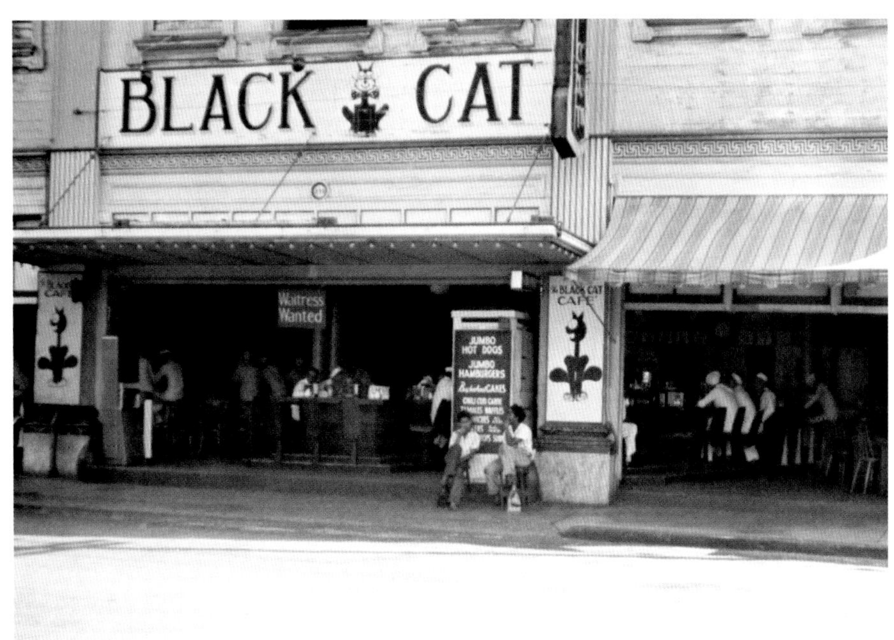
BLACK CAT
Waitress Wanted
JUMBO HOT DOGS
JUMBO HAMBURGERS
CAKES
BLACK CAT CAFE

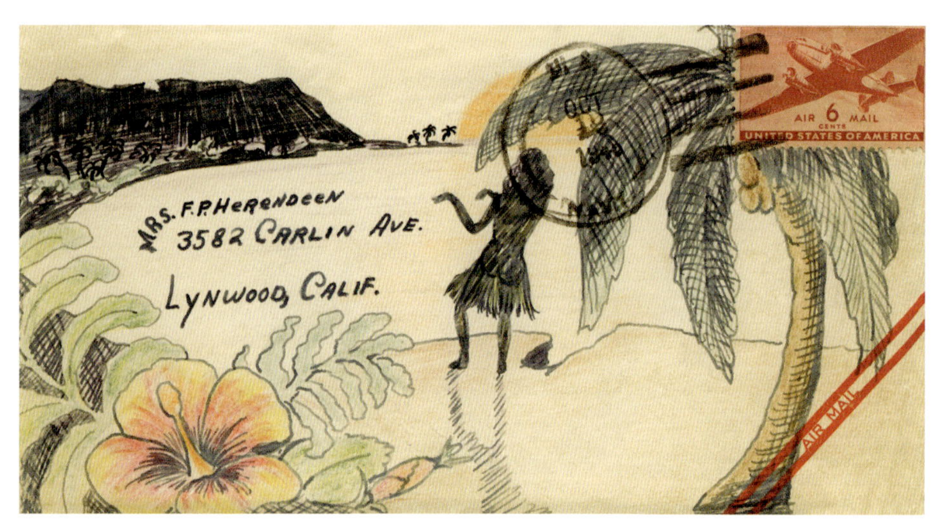
MRS. F.P. Herendeen
3582 Carlin Ave.
Lynwood, Calif.
AIR 6 MAIL
CENTS
UNITED STATES OF AMERICA
AIR MAIL

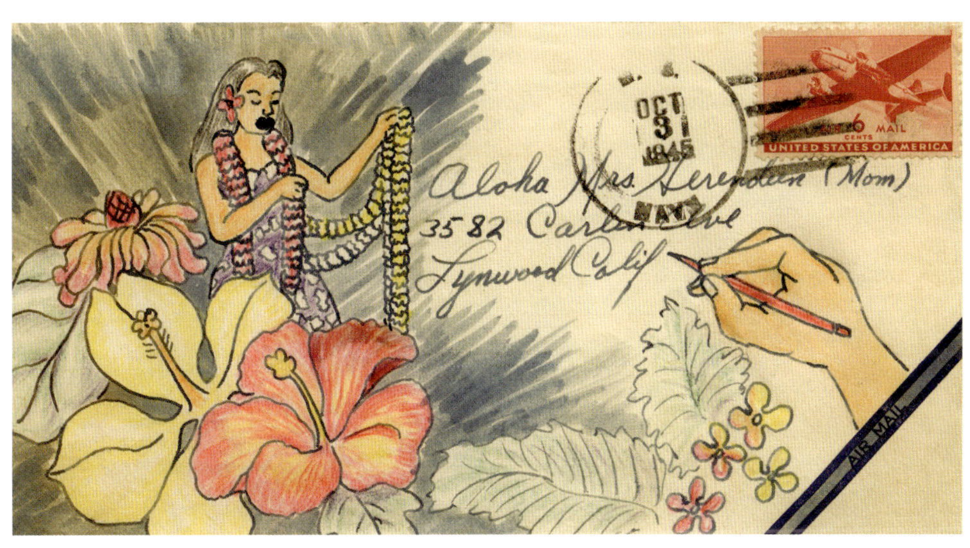
OCT
31
1945
NAVY
6 CENTS MAIL
UNITED STATES OF AMERICA
Aloha
(Mom)
Lynwood Calif
AIR MAIL

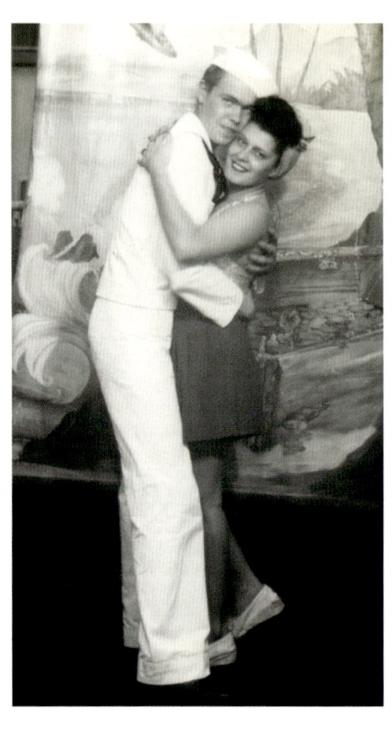

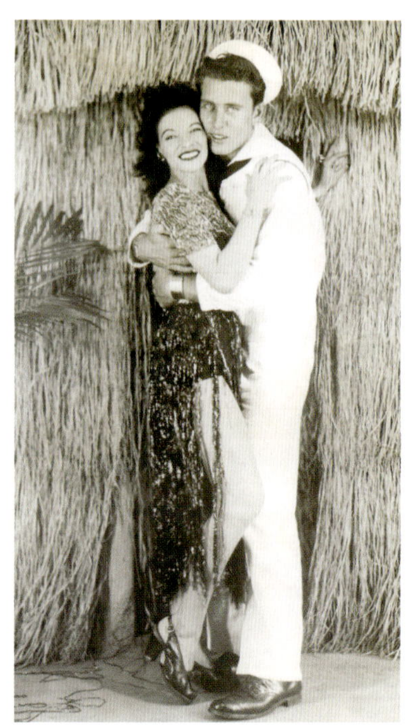

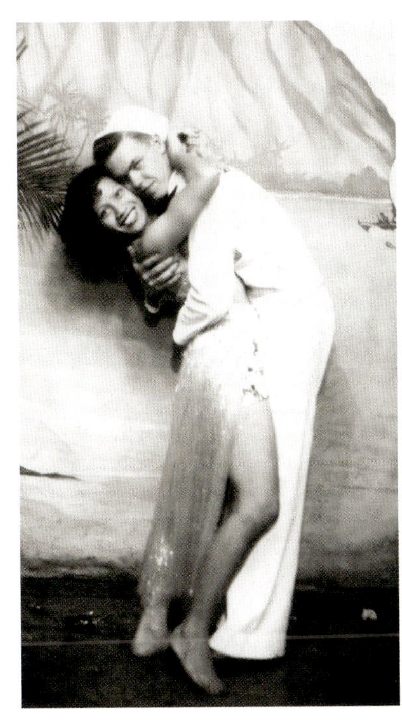

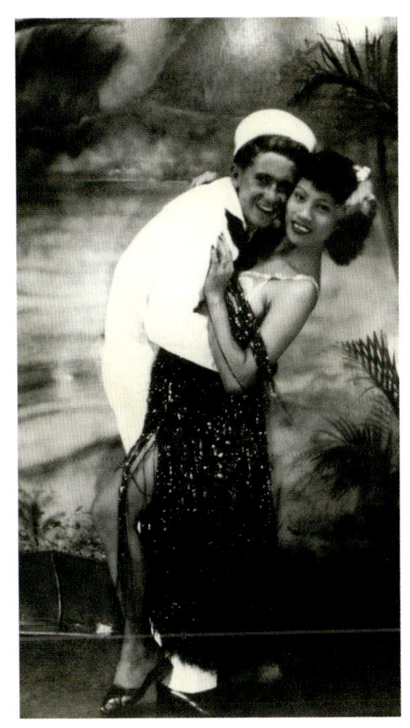

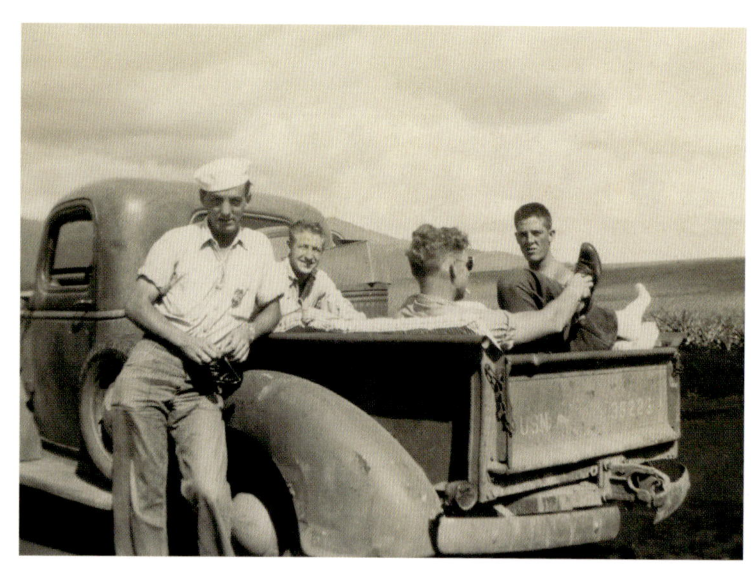
USN

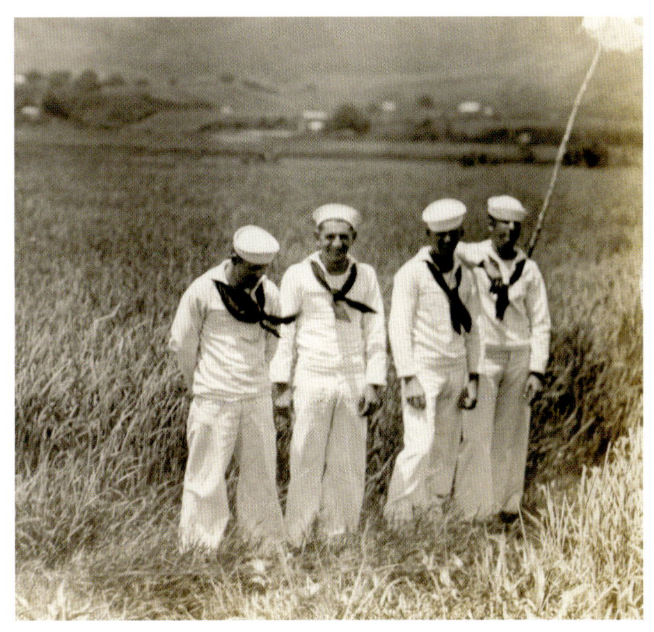

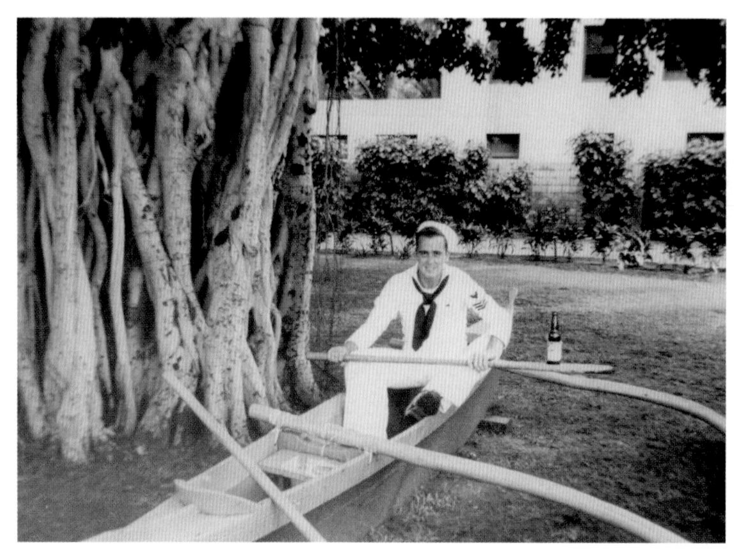

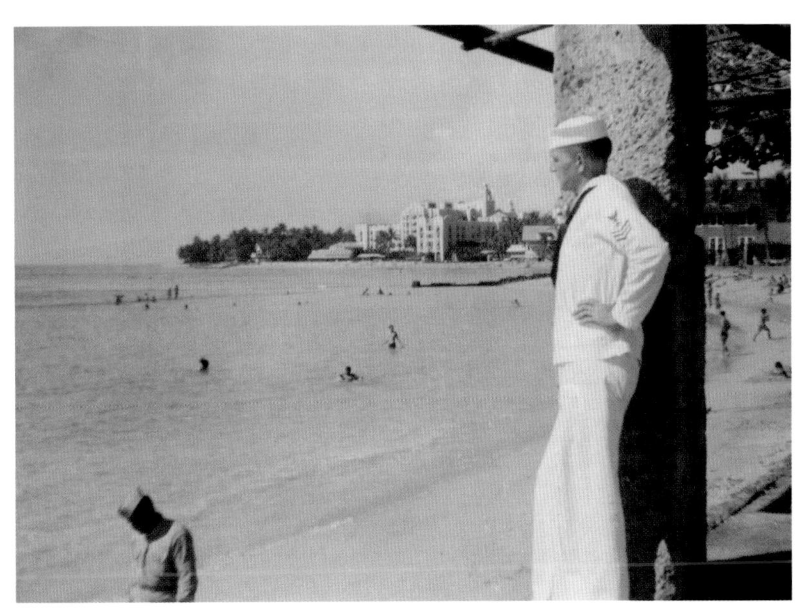

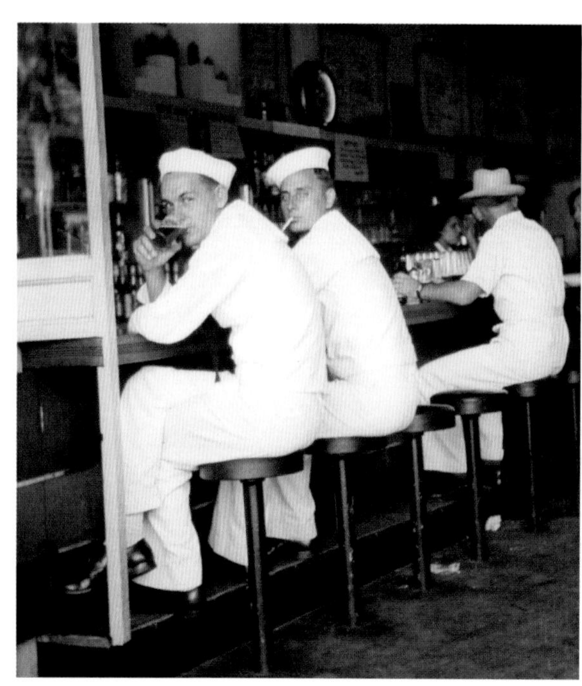

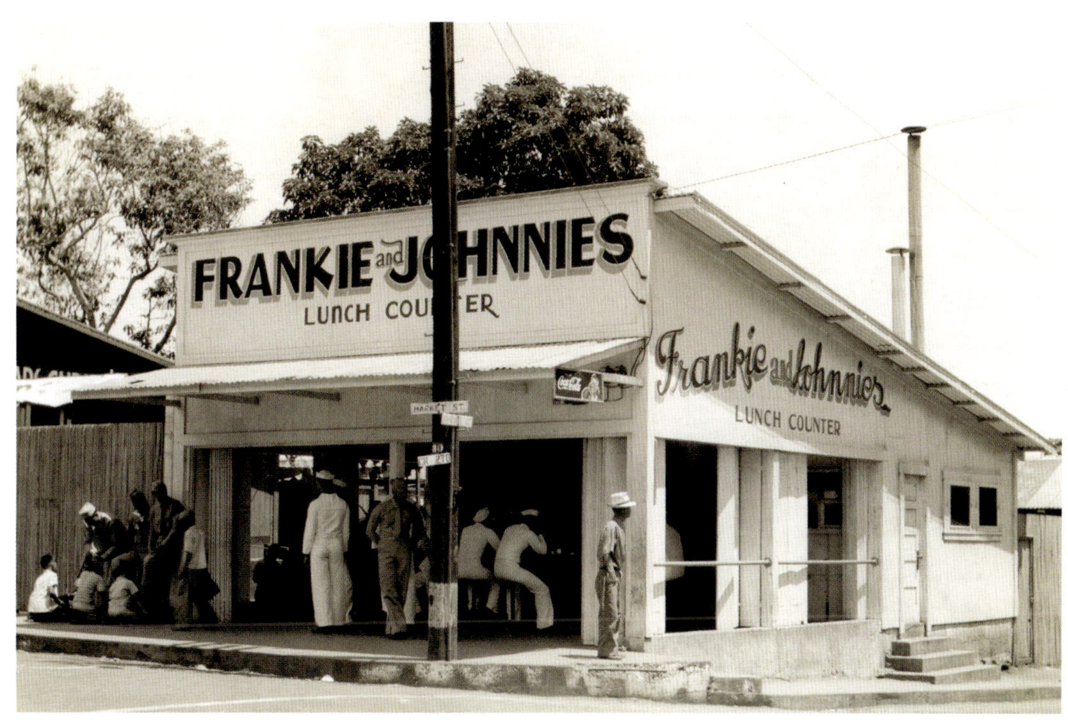
FRANKIE and JOHNNIES
LUNCH COUNTER
Frankie and Johnnies
LUNCH COUNTER

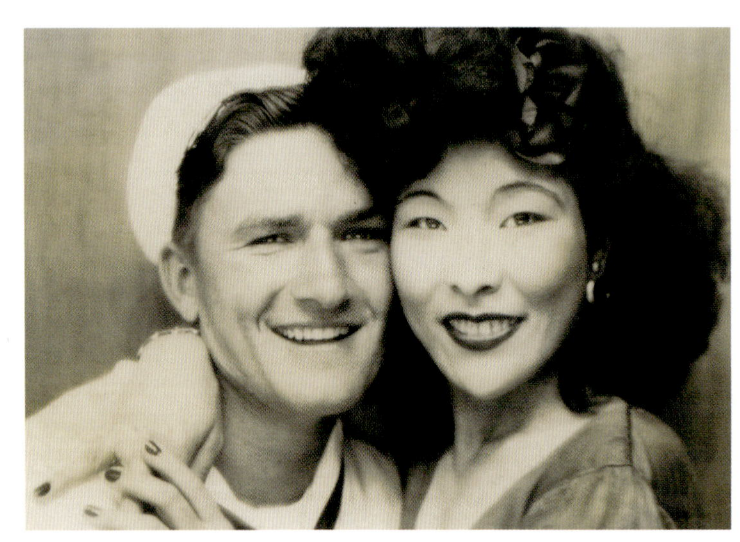

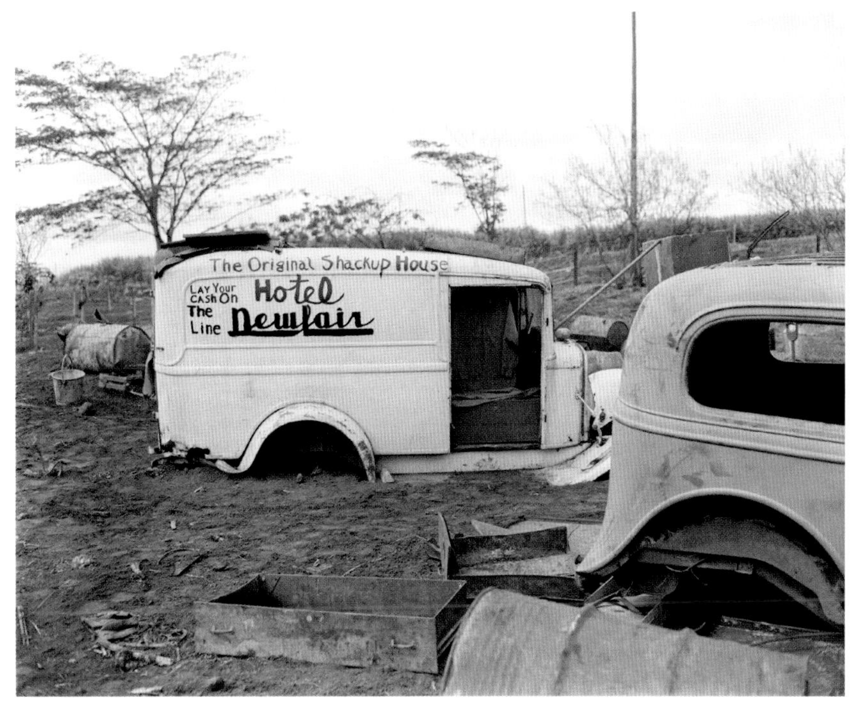
The Original Shackup House
LAY Your CASH On The Line
Hotel
Dewlair

ARMY TRANSPORT SERVICE
HONOLULU
PASS TO BOARD TRANSPORT

....
(Name)

and .... Others

Date ....

PASS TO BE TAKEN UP AT GANGPLANK

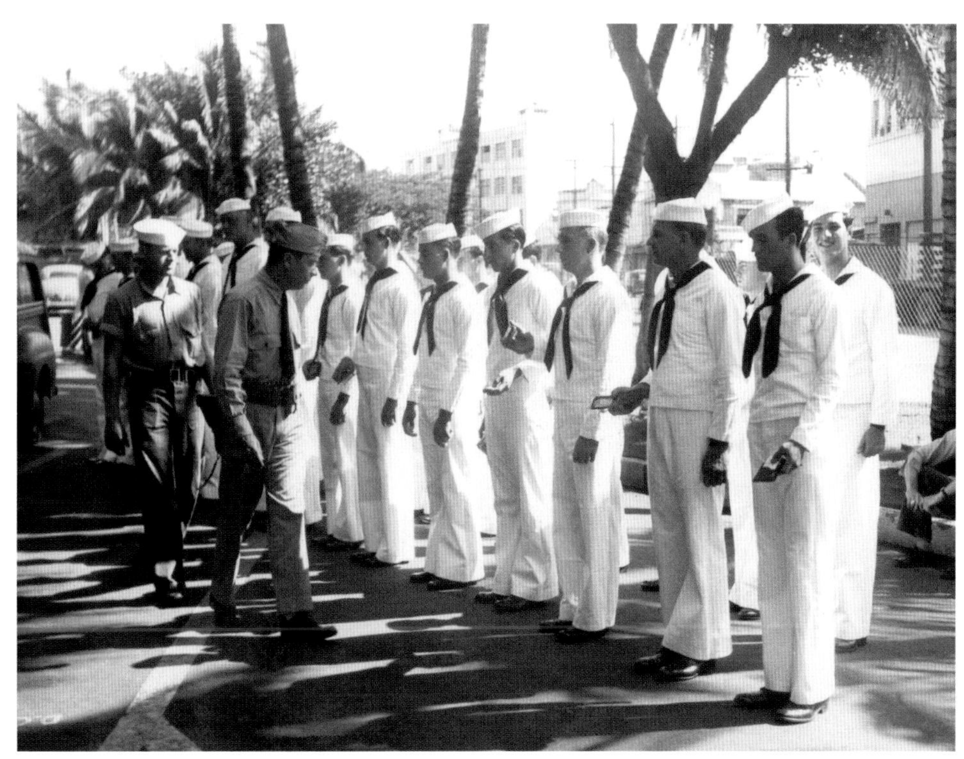

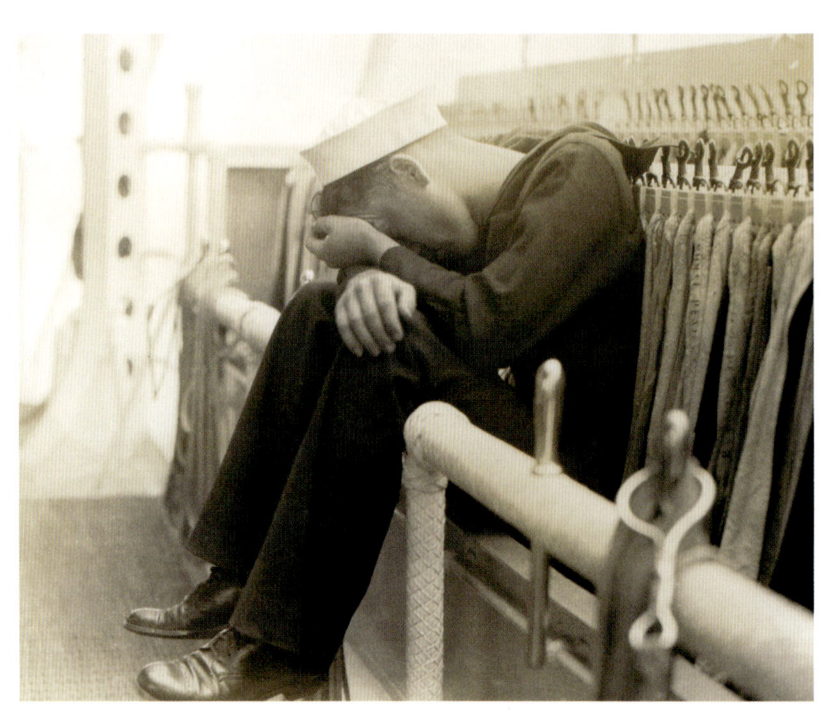

All images are from the Jim Heimann Collection unless otherwise noted.

Arizona State Library 71; Ray Jerome Baker, Bishop Museum 40; Laurence Hata, Bishop Museum (cropped from original) 46; Kodak Hawaii, Bishop Museum 50; Tai Sing Loo, Bishop Museum (cropped from original) 54; James Summerlin, Bishop Museum 41; Hawaii State Archives 6, 28; National Archives 8, 51, 66, 68, 83; University of Hawaii at Manoa Library 36, 63

Distributed Art Publishers, Inc. www.artbook.com

Printed in China

ISBN 978-0-9916198-1-8

Stewed,

screwed,

and tattooed